THE LAST KNOT

THE LAST KNOT

SHABIR AHMAD MIR

MACMILLAN

First published 2025 by Macmillan
an imprint of Pan Macmillan Publishing India Private Limited
707 Kailash Building
26 K. G. Marg, New Delhi 110001
www.panmacmillan.co.in

Pan Macmillan, The Smithson, 6 Briset Street, Farringdon, London EC1M 5NR
Associated companies throughout the world
www.panmacmillan.com

ISBN 978-93-6113-819-5

1 3 5 7 9 8 6 4 2

Typeset in Guardi LT Std by R. Ajith Kumar, New Delhi
Printed and bound in India by Thomson Press India Ltd.

FSC www.fsc.org MIX Paper | Supporting responsible forestry FSC® C010615

For Arwah
[who wasn't around last time]

And the usual suspects.
[Mariam, Aiman, Huzi, Hamza]

'Old father, old artificer, stand me now and ever in good stead.'

– JAMES JOYCE, *A Portrait of the Artist as a Young Man*

1

The Mountains

I open my eyes and see the undulating expanse of the water spread before me. Dal – the lake, blue. So blue ... An inverted sky ... My eyes, like a pair of birds, fly over this sky. Across it. Beyond it. Till the mountains rise. Abrupt. Adamant. They let nothing pass, these mountains. I turn to my right. There they are again, the mountains ... Cold. Callous ... As they are on my left too ... Implacable. Immovable ...

With a shiver, cold as a centipede, running down my spine, I slowly – very slowly – turn back. The mountains stare back at me. Foreboding. Forewarning.

The omnipotence of the mountains is complete.

The only way out, I tell myself, is to fly over them. Yes, fly ... Fly, fly ... Fly, fly ... Fly, fly ... Fly, fly ... The word and the thought, trapped in my head, gallop to break free like a horse out of his burning stable.

And drag me, drag me away from the lake. Away and up the hillock of Haer Parbat, way past Kallai – the wall – through its presumptuous gateway. Inside: a meandering street that now turns into a lane and now a by-lane. Drag me to the door of our karkhan, our workshop.

I stand at the door listening to the sing-song of the wusteh, my master, reciting the taalim.

'*Czor karus gulaeb, baey karus akh zangaer, baey karus akh sabz. Trey karus anaer* (four knots of light pink, then one knot of bottle green, two knots of green then three knots of pomegranate red) ...' Wusteh sings. His words a command, his voice a tradition.

'*Adsa* (as you say) ...' the apprentices sing back; their voices affirming their acquiescence as their fingers, no longer bound by their will, sway to the chants of the wusteh's song. The fingers working in tandem like bewitched silkworms who must suck on the threads of the weft balls hanging from the loom and then squirm – nimbly, adroitly – back and forth, across the white warp threads stretched tightly into a frame on the loom, before the khour – the knife – comes down with a swift motion to cut off the weft thread and leave it tied as a knot on the loom. Knot after knot they tie, as they have been tied before, as they will be tied long after. The hands keep on changing but the knots remain the same. The song of the taalim makes sure of that.

The master sings, the apprentices obey and this duet on the loom continues in mellifluous monotony and agonizing repetition for months, if not years; each day adding just a barely perceptible but excruciating layer of colour and shape on the loom, as if one were measuring out the void of eternity in handfuls ...

Till one day when the master and his apprentices wake up at the end of eternity to find that the knots that they have been tying are knots no more; instead, it is a carpet that has blossomed on their loom. The bittersweet fruit of their labour leaves them unsure of their own purpose for some time before they start it all again. The taalim. The knots. Again and again. An eternity of eternities unravelling on the loom.

I walk in. Wusteh continues his chant. The apprentices continue their obedience. The loom, insouciant. My entry makes no difference to this self-serving universe of knots and hands.

I walk over to the corner of the room where a half-woven carpet, like a rotting corpse hung upside down, is stretched across the frame of a smaller loom. I start to remove the warp from the upper roller. From the corner of his eye, Wusteh has seen this catastrophe. He stops his chanting. The hands come to a halt. The knots suspended. The apprentices aghast. Everything bought to a grinding standstill. The Universe is disturbed.

Wusteh gets up from his loom and rushes to me. 'What the hell are you doing?' he cries in a voice whose ugly, breathless pitch is completely at odds with the sing-song in which he was chanting the taalim just a moment earlier. 'Stop it! What madness is this? That carpet there, it is almost half done, why are you unravelling the labour of all these months? What is wrong with you?'

I remove the rotting corpse of the undone carpet from the loom.

'All those knots gone to waste! What in God's name are you up to?'

I can see white flecks of snow in the brown of my wusteh's eyes as I tell him, 'I am going to weave a carpet that will fly.'

2

The Pebble

In the beginning, it was water. Water, water all around. Only water. As if someone had tied knot after knot of water till the carpet of water had overflown its loom and spread itself all around and everywhere. Water that was grey in the winter morning, blue in the summer noon and, sometimes, green in the spring evening. Water that gurgled in laughter and tiptoed on a ripple as it explored its own immense solitude and sang strange songs of longing when it rained. Water that told its own story to itself in its guttural voice, sang a lullaby to itself when it grew too dark. Night after day. Night after night.

Water that delighted in each knot of its being as it discovered the miracle that was its existence.

Water that, impregnated of its own happiness, bore two sons. Tsand and Mond. Two big-boned, immense babies whose giant guffaws could be heard for miles from the shores of the Water in whose proud womb they swam incessantly. Tsand and Mond, whose joy and large laughter frightened the men that had just arrived on the shore to lay claim to the land by the Water. Men who prayed to the gods that they had brought with them to tame the Water and exorcise it of its monsters before they consecrated it for eternity. The gods whose trident of anger is roused in all its phallic fury and out flies a Haer – a sparrow – from their loins. The Sparrow that picks up a pebble and drops it like a curse from the immense height of its power and contempt. The pebble that, like the sentence of a tyrant, grows in its wrath as it falls all the way down onto the Water. The Water whose liquid ribs break under the weight of the engorged pebble and fails to protect her Tsand. Tsand, who lays buried under the pebble, groaning, his words no more than empty bubbles floating away …

With each dying breath of Tsand, the pebble grows. Grows and grows and grows till it becomes a rigid knot across time and space, till it becomes a parbat – a giant rock. A hill. Haer Parbat. The Hill of Sparrow. And centuries of history gather all around this hill like moss on a stone.

Proud as a tombstone, the hill stood with all its moss when the Great Emperor from the plains beyond the mountains arrived. Let us start history anew, he decreed. Let us built a new city on Haer Parbat, he decided. For the city that knelt before him, with all its history and moss, was nothing more than the spoils of war; and the spoils of war always belong to the victor. Thus, the Great Emperor builds a wall all around the Hill of Sparrow to demarcate this new city – this new history – from the old one that remained sprawled around the meandering waters of the river Jhelum. Ka'lai, people called this wall, and lured by the safety that walls conjure, some of the more wretched ones moved inside, only to find that it was all the same both within the wall and beyond it. Those wretched ones found that new histories, new cities, are just mirages born of the skeletons of the old ones. And centuries later, when a governor of another emperor builds a fort atop the hill with its own set of walls, all that the people would see would be one more folly of history. One more spoil to one more victor.

The fort changes hands after intervals of time as new victors ride to its door. But no matter whose time it is, the fort itself always perches like a vulture on the top of Haer Parbat, digging its talons deep, deep into the flesh of memory as well as the body of the hill. The only solace one can find on this tormented hill is the shrine of Makhdoom Saab, just below the fort, on the southern slope.

Up this hill I climb. To the shrine of Makhdoom Saab I climb. Breath by slow breath I climb. I heave. I pant. I breathe in gasps. But I climb and climb. My chest tightens. Something heavy churns within me. Thick, heavy; I want to vomit so badly. My heart pumps fear and pain. I try to run. But my legs refuse; the ground beneath them waxes and wanes into a web of taut, tired threads. A cobweb! A familiar cobweb! A loom! A loom! I stand on my loom!

Weave.

A spider sings as I fall on my knees and sink deep, deep ...

... one knot of ash grey, three knots of fiery red ...

I dig in my nails and try to break free.

... For God's sake, weave!

I kick back with all I have. Away from that cobweb. Away from my loom, away from that web of fecund sterility. Away from the thousand knots that I have done and undone.

... Something. Anything. One knot of sweat. Three knots of blood ...

I dig in with my nails and drag myself up. Drag, drag, drag ... Up, up, up ...

We can't stop weaving! Nobody can. What shall we tell them?

If I stop now, I am lost. Trapped in this cobweb and lost forever. The web will eat me up. The spider is waiting.

... My God! My God! You will be the ruin of us all ...

Up, up. Drag. Up. Up. There, there the shrine beckons to me. Save me, please! Grab me. Lift me. Drag me up there. Please. Just a little more. There, there. Almost there ...

Heaving, panting, I lie besides the tomb of my saint, my Makhdoom Saab.

'Ya Sheikh Hamza Makhdoomi!' I cry aloud and weep.

A loud burst of cannon fire rings through the helpless air. It is the fort announcing it is midday. They even control the time, I tell myself as I gather my arms around myself and weep anew.

I weep between the walls, with mountains all around me. A Mond atop Haer Parbat and the Tsand underneath it.

3

The Cave

Outside the shrine of Makhdoom Saab, the slope of Haer Parbat juts out like a giant pouting lip. A man stands there, on this lip of hill, throwing grains at pigeons that coo and peck all around him. There is something about the way he throws the handfuls of grains at the pigeons – something stunted, something restricted. There is something about his hands ... something ... something missing ... the thumbs? Ah yes, the thumbs! He does not have them. Four fingers and a stub on both his hands. The man looks at me, catches me staring at his hands, but doesn't flinch. He does not withdraw his hands inside his sleeves. He proudly displays the stubs of his thumbs. 'Looking at them?' he asks me with a voice that demands respect. I blush. 'A man with no thumbs, you understand what that means?'

'You cannot weave,' I cry out loud without meaning to.

The man smiles. A bittersweet smile like a hailstorm on a summer noon. 'Not anymore,' the words escape his lips. Now he looks at my hands, at my thumbs. 'Hmmm ... So you are a weaver?'

I nod.

'A weaver, indeed! And what sort of weaver are you if you are not at your loom at this time of the day?' he asks me with a sneer. 'Pray, tell me,' the man says as he points towards the fort at the top of the hillock, 'have they really grown so soft that they allow their weavers to roam around in the middle of the day? What about your wusteh? Is he an imperial son-in-law or does he enjoy lashings? Or has he found some treasure to pay for your absence? Or is it ... wait, is that it? You have run away from your karkhan. That is it, isn't it?'

I shake my head. 'No, I didn't run away.'

'I hope you are telling the truth and I pray it is so. You understand that you cannot run away? The fort will find you. It always does – whosoever it be and wheresoever he runs. Between these mountains, there is no escape.'

'My wusteh sent me here.'

'What?!'

'My wusteh sent me here. To you. To Abli Bab.'

'Which wusteh?'

I tell him the name.

'So the good old wusteh sends his apprentice to me. To the thumbless Abli Bab of all people. Things must be pretty serious. Ha ha ha ha …' The man lets out a roar of laughter as his fingers comb his luxurious white beard that hangs like tufts of carded cotton from his chin and cheeks.

'Come,' he leads me to a small cave cut into the side of Haer Parbat, a little below the shrine. The cave's mouth, a winding slit running across the rocks of the hill, makes the cave invisible to anyone who does not know of its existence. Inside, he makes me sit on a woollen felt spread over the straw strewn across the floor, while he lights up the chillum of his jajeer. As the tobacco fumes up and starts to fill the cave, Abli Bab asks me, 'So now, what brings you here?'

I don't know what to say. 'The loom is a web,' I say anyhow. 'And I am trapped. Week after sterile week I have spent at the loom now, but to no gain. The wusteh recites the taalim but my hands refuse to acquiesce. Not that I don't want to tie those knots, but I just can't. No matter how hard I try, I just cannot. The knots that he wants me to tie wither away before my hands can tie them on the loom.'

That is all I manage to say. I don't have any more words. I don't know what more to say. It is over to Abli Bab now. But Abli Bab says nothing. He just sucks on his jajeer. He sucks on his jajeer forcefully, as if his life depended on it. He sucks and spews out a whorl of smoke from his mouth. The smoke wafts around for a brief moment before it vanishes, leaving behind only a faint promise of sleep and whispers. Abli Bab sucks more and more, cascades of smoke – blue and grey – pour out of his mouth and nostrils, filling up the whole cave. The promise grows stronger and stronger. It is all around now, the smoke, as is the promise. It fills up everything. It overcomes everything. There is nothing else to breathe now. The flood of smoke rushes into my lungs and suddenly, a sun explodes inside my head. I am all smoke and light now. Inside and outside. It is all whispers and sleep now. I, Abli Bab, this cave, this hill, this universe ... nothing but a conspiracy of whispers. Suddenly, words, like serpents, uncoil and dart all around. *Weave ... A carpet that will fly ... weave, for God's sake, weave ... What if they find out that you are no longer weaving ... one knot of ash grey, three knots of fiery red ... Do you want to fly? ... Fly. Fly. Fly ... weave ... But you can't. They won't let you ... weave ... Something. Anything ... One knot of sweat. Three knots of blood ... how can you? ... WEAVE ... How will you?*

... The mountains ... the fort ... they will find out, they always do ... WEAVE ... There is no hiding from them, there never is ... They will flay us all ... WEAVE ... My God, you will be the ruin of us all ... WEAVE. WEAVE. WEAVE ... Only that word remains now – weave. It fills the cavity of the cave like an interminable echo – the rattle of a giant on his deathbed. I slap my ears shut; they are about to burst.

'Here, here. Drink this,' the voice of Abli Bab pierces through the smoke and whispers like the wail of a banshee through the night. I gulp the water down. Abli Bab is sitting in front of me. He is talking to me. He has been talking to me. The smoke clears and his words gently waft into my ears. Slowly, I begin to register them, to understand them. '... not possible in a karkhan. Not while they have eyes there. Sooner or later, they will find out and once they do, the punishment would be brutal and swift, but it will not be just for you. And that is the worst and cruellest part of it all. Your wụsteh understands that. That is why he sent you here, that wily old bastard. Only Abli Bab has nothing to lose. Damn him! And that too right here, under the nose of the fort! What audacity! Be that as it may, you will stay with me. And I will try to help in whatever way I can.'

4

The Star

'It is said that Solomon had a carpet that would fly,' the voice of Abli Bab floats into my ears at the break of dawn. We stand on the ledge of Haer Parbat. He tries to feed pigeons while I watch over the buds of light that have just started to blossom on the shrinking tendrils of the vanishing night. Beneath us, away from Haer Parbat, the old city is curled up on either bank of the river Jhelum in a deep and obstinate sleep. Tiny, blue-black hands of the nascent morning knock at its ashen doors, but the tired city refuses to wake up.

'A carpet that would take him to any place anytime,' Abli Bab continues as his silhouette and his voice grow sharper. 'Now the carpet, it is said, was just one among many that Solomon had. That is to say, it wasn't different from any other fine carpet of its time. Just blue silk knotted and tied neatly. Pretty to look at, but nothing extraordinary. Nothing to mark it for flight in itself. It was rather the wind that carried it, made it fly. You see, Solomon was a mighty prophet and the Lord Almighty had granted him dominion over wind as He, in His infinite grace and wisdom, had granted Solomon dominion over water and jinns and animals as well. Solomon, with the leave of the Almighty, would command the wind to carry him over and the wind would abide. It would lift the carpet with Solomon on it and take them to wherever Solomon commanded,' Abli Bab finishes as he wipes his hands on his fheran. He is done with the pigeons. Now he turns towards me. His eyes – two simmering, black suns – burn into me, raising questions, asking me: *What dominion has been granted to you? Which wind is subjugated to your command?* None, my eyes plead back. Absolutely none! But his eyes keep on probing, keep on asking; growing bigger and blacker, choking the dawn all around me.

Just then, the sky cracks open with an ugly thunderous clap. It is the howl of the fort above us. They have fired the cannon to announce the start of the day. Scared, the pigeons fly away. Abli Bab looks at them wistfully, his eyes no longer on me. 'But ...' he says as he looks up at the pigeons circling around before they fly away, 'some say it was the carpet that flew.' The fluttering wings of the fleeing pigeons stifle

Abli Bab's voice. I walk closer to hear him better. 'For it wasn't just any carpet. It was rather a special one. A special gift from the Queen of Sheba to Solomon. The alchemists at the Queen's court had wrought a miracle. They had created a dye that worked wonders. A dye that didn't yield to its handler's command easily but, once it did, it was pure magic. A carpet knotted from the yarn soaked in this dye would be light as a feather and buoyant as a cloud. A carpet that would fly. A carpet that the Queen of Sheba gifted to Solomon.' The last pigeon flies away, leaving behind Abli Bab standing over pigeon droppings and moulted feathers.

Abli Bab turns to me once again. A faint smile upturns the corners of his lips. 'Most of them do not believe in Sheba's gift. It is blasphemy, they say. After all, alchemists supplanting divine dominion is nothing but sacrilege.' The smile is all over Abli Bab's face now. It has even crept into his eyes. 'Sacrilege or submission. The choice is yours.'

But is it? Do I really have a choice in all this? Did I choose to suffer like this? Can I choose anything else but an end to this suffering? Can anyone ever choose anything but an end to their suffering? The choice, if any, is already made; it always is. One look at me and Abli Bab sees that I am way past the illusion that he is calling a choice. 'But it seems that your choice is already made,' he says, 'Be that as it may. Now then, hear me and hear me good. It is a fact well known to all that Solomon's sigil was a star. His signet bore it and it carried his royal command. And those who know will tell you this as well that Solomon's treasures were never truly lost at all. As nothing is ever truly lost. Things tend to scatter themselves around us till time makes their presence oblivious. So oblivious that we no longer see them for what they really are. That is how treasures hide in plain sight. That is how Solomon's treasures are hiding in plain sight. And whoever seeks them, let him be guided by the Solomon's star. Find the star and perchance, it may lead you to what you seek,' he says as I walk past him, over to the edge of the ledge.

A shiver passes through the old city spread before me, as if someone had untied the knot that was the night. The pleas of dawn may have failed but the fort's canonical command is not to be ignored. The old city is waking up. The houses are stretching themselves with yawns. The hearths are lit and blue smoke rises up like sighs. The doors open. Women come out. And the Jhelum finds a way into their houses – in pots and pitchers balanced on hips and heads as they sway down and back up the stairs cut into the banks of the river. As pitchers fill up, lips drooling with the spittle of gossip spill the whispers of the night and rumours of the day before on these steps of the yaarbal. Yaar – friend – and bal – place: a place for friends. A friendly place. A nice place to eavesdrop on this city's secrets. A nice place to start looking for stars.

'Remember, you can always come back here if need be,' Abli Bab says as he walks up to me from behind. He takes the turban from my head and tears the collar of my fheran. He takes pigeon droppings and moulted feathers from the ground and smears them all over my face and chest and rubs some of it into my hair as he keeps talking. 'News from the karkhan says that your absence has already drawn the attention of the fort. The wusteh has been making excuses for you. He has had it declared that you went crazy with the knots and consequently, you are of no use at the loom. But you know them, you very well know those relentless hounds of the fort. If madness were a way out, I believe everyone out here would have gone crazy already. They have made the wusteh pledge his son in your place at the karkhan. That will take care of their loss. But that doesn't mean they will let you go if they can help it. They will be looking for you everywhere, just to be sure. They trust no one. But since you must go to the old city down there, your only chance at survival is to play along. You are officially mad now, so you must look mad, talk mad, smell mad. That and some luck may get you through. Don't give them an excuse to tear you apart limb from limb. Believe me, they don't need much of an excuse anyway. Remember my words and go now. Farewell.'

5

The Pitcher

She dips her clay pitcher into the Jhelum. Water gurgles in. As she stoops over the rapidly filling pitcher, a lock of hair tucked behind her left ear jumps at the chance and sets itself free. Exasperated, she tries to restrain the wayward lock with the rest of her hair that has been knotted into a tight plait under the piece of cloth tied around her head. But it tumbles out again, this little lock of hair that refuses to be knotted and, instead, hangs by her cheek like an obstinate lover desperate for kisses. Suddenly, she looks up and catches me staring at her. Our eyes lock for a brief moment. I cannot bear it. I cannot bear looking into those eyes lest all my pretence is gone. I break contact. I look away. I look up at the leaves of the chinar tree. Pumped up with spring blood, the leaves are a resplendent green as I sit under them, stinking of pigeon shit and my own.

How long have I been sitting here? How long have I been at this yaarbal? I sigh and look down again only to find she is there, standing in front of me. Her pitcher balanced on her right shoulder and her left hand on her hip, she looks as if she is about to break into a merry dance.

'What do you keep staring at?'

This is not the first time she has caught me looking, but this is the first time she has walked up to me. 'Tell me, what do you keep staring at?' she repeats.

Promise of Spring, I would have said if I weren't mad. '*Tuh*,' I spit on her face in reply instead. A cackle of laughter rises up from the yaarbal. 'That should be enough to wash her face,' one of the women cries out loud. 'Or maybe that would fetch her a groom finally,' someone else adds. The laughter redoubles.

She is livid. Blood rushes to her oblong face, forcing it to turn from soft beige to a muddy red. She wants to hit me. She really does. Her lithe frame shakes against itself as she violently restrains herself. She cannot hit me. She just cannot, no matter how much she wants to. I am a man. And a moutt – a crazy one – at that. She is just a girl. Her anger might overcome her age, but it cannot overcome her sex. She realizes that much despite her blinding rage. She turns away from me, the braid of her knotted hair lashing angrily across the dainty curve of her back as she stomps away to her house, a few paces across the yaarbal. She will come out again. She must. One or two pitchers of water are enough for a day's cooking and drinking; enough for most women out here at the yaarbal. But not for this one, the one with the unruly lock of hair. She must come out again. I know she will come out again. The whispers at the yaarbal have told me everything about her. She has to come out again and again. As she does every morning. She must carry pitcher after pitcher of water to fill up her father's cauldron. She must fill up that big copper cauldron for her father, the rangur – the dyer – to stir up the alchemy of colours. The alchemy of red, green, yellow and all the other hues whose secrets have been passed on to him from his father, who in turn inherited them from his own father. Some secrets that one or another father stumbled upon in a moment of pure madness. Some secrets that a lifetime was not enough to unravel and could only be discovered by a succession of sons, as son after son circumvented his father's mortality. Some secrets that a great-great-grandfather might have eavesdropped on as some blasphemous alchemist raged aloud in his dungeon.

Secrets of all kinds that have been shaped into traditions on Time's anvil and passed on as inheritance, like the cauldrons themselves. Secrets that keep diluting themselves at the gossiping steps of the yaarbal.

She walks out again, as I knew she would. But this time, she has brought along her father as well. She almost drags him to me.

'This is what you brought me out for?' the rangur says incredulously, pointing towards me. 'He is a moutt, for God's sake. A crazy man. He is supposed to stare and spit at people. And you are supposed to avoid him. Besides, the Jhelum has enough water to clean all the spittle of the world, doesn't it? What is the big deal? Now go and fetch water. The cauldrons are not going to fill up themselves, are they? For God's sake, Heemal, hurry up. Haven't we wasted enough time this morning already?' He has no time to lose, he repeats again and again. He is about to go back to his house.

Heemal, the one with the unruly lock, is aghast. She looks at her father and then she looks at me, the feeling of disbelief painted a dark red on her cheeks. Betrayed, anger uncoils in her belly and rises into her head; it slithers into her mouth. She can no longer control it; it takes over, the anger. She spits at me with the vehemence of a snake. The effort sends tremors up her body. Shaking, she turns away from me violently, and the pitcher slips from her grasp. She reaches out reflexively to catch the pitcher in mid-air before it hits the steps of the yaarbal. But all she manages to do is to stumble and trip over. She goes crashing down the yaarbal. The pitcher survives somehow and lands safely in the Jhelum, while she ends up on her back across the steps at the bottom of the yaarbal.

She tries to get up.

She cannot.

She is in pain. Her cries vouch for it.

I see my chance and I jump at it. I refuse to be tucked under the chinar tree any longer. I almost tumble down the steps. I am at her side as quickly as I can be, but I don't know what to do. I just reach out for the pitcher and hold it for her while she writhes in pain.

'What a terrible morning!' her father cries from the top of the steps. He rushes down and tries to get his daughter back on her feet. But he can't. Her left foot is not right. She winces as she tries to stand up. She tries again, but the pain overwhelms her. She gives up.

'A terrible, terrible morning!' her father cries as he slaps his forehead. 'What is to be done now? Who will fetch the water?' He keeps on murmuring as he slips his arm under Heemal's shoulders and hoists her up. She climbs up the stairs supported by her father, hopping on her right foot, and slowly limps away to her house. 'Who will fetch the water?' her father keeps repeating all the way to their house. 'Who will fetch the water?'

I follow them with the pitcher of water in my hands.

6

The Cauldron

Every morning, we start with the small cauldron, Heemal and I. Not the old copper one with a star inscribed on its neck, but the smaller bronze one. Pitcher after pitcher of water we pour into it till the rangur says enough and starts to wash undyed yarn in it. Most of the times it is wool, sometimes it is silk. 'The yarn must be pure before we start to impurify it,' he chuckles lecherously as he repeats the old dictum of his trade.

'That is no joke,' Heemal tells her father, 'but a great piece of advice from our forefathers.'

'Of course that is not a joke, but you are,' the rangur snarls back. 'You, whose unmarried self is the greatest burden on my forefathers' graves, and yet you have the gall to think that you know my forefathers better than I do – what greater joke can there be?

Anger, pain and humiliation wrestle in Heemal's eyes for an answer, but silence trumps them all. She picks up her pitcher and walks out. I follow her.

Outside, she sits under the chinar. Alone. Lonely.

I sit by her side. The pretence of my madness shrivels at the touch of the cold sadness that surrounds her like autumn mist.

'It is all a joke for him,' she says with a voice that freezes my heart. 'He doesn't understand it. That is not just some useless piece of wit passed on by our forefathers. A dye, any dye, is an impurity forced upon the fibre. Our ancestors knew that, as any dyer worth his salt would. The yarn must be pure before we make it impure. That is as good a lesson as any. Lesson, mind you, not some vulgar joke. You see, only that yarn which is pure will put on a colour you want it to. Otherwise, the impurity within resists the impurity forced upon it and the result is only as good as anybody's guess. You dye an impure yarn pomegranate red and it comes out brown as a cinnamon stick. And what sort of a dyer are you if you do not even know what colour your yarn would end up with?'

I have been hanging on to her words with eyes and mouth wide open. She looks at my face and breaks out into wild laughter. 'You crazy beast! Look at you, as if you understood any part of it. What luck! What life! A lout for a father and a moutt to share my grief with!'

'Moutt. Moutt ... I am a moutt ...' I say.

'Indeed, you are. You stinking donkey. Now get up and get going. Nobody is going to do your donkey work for you. *Fetch the water, donkey, fetch the water,'* she sings the last sentence in a prim falsetto.

'Donkey. Donkey,' I repeat. My voice hoarse as that of a frog in the rain. She laughs. The mist clears. I laugh. We both laugh. And we keep chuckling as we carry our pitchers of water inside. 'It is time to fill up the big copper cauldron now,' the rangur says with a gesture. The one with a star inscribed on its neck and kept over the hearth. We go out and fetch more water while the rangur kindles a fire in the hearth as he keeps mumbling angrily about his forefathers. He keeps getting angrier as we pour pitcher after pitcher of water into the cauldron, chuckling all along our way in and out. The fire lights up. The water starts to boil. It is time.

The rangur walks to his tin containers sitting in rows on wood shelves hanging on the wall. These tin containers are filled with powders of all hues. From pomegranate rinds to wild madder roots, from walnut kernels to sap collected from willow trees – colours extracted, dried, pulverized and reduced to dust. Rainbows imprisoned in tin containers waiting to be set free into the boiling tempest of the cauldron.

'My daughter thinks she knows my forefathers better than I,' the rangur says to everyone and no one as he opens a container and takes out a handful of powder from it. 'She thinks she is truer to my trade and to the trade of my forefathers than I will ever be,' the rangur continues as he considers the powder carefully, weighing it with his right hand. It isn't enough, he decides. He adds some more to it. He considers it again. 'But shouldn't she rather be concerned about her own self? Here she is, in this house, when she should have been married already, living with her husband by now. Each passing day does not make her any younger. The whispers at the yaarbal and the smirks of the neighbours – that is what should keep her awake at night and worried during the day. She ought to leave the forefathers and dyeing to me.' The words leave pits in the air all around like bear traps in the woods. The rangur drops the powder into the boiling water. He now turns and looks at Heemal. His gloating eyes trying to challenge her to respond before he insults her more, to goad her to walk into his trap. But Heemal refuses to turn around. Instead, she walks up to the shelves on the wall and picks up a container, a small one at the end of the second shelf. She takes out a fistful of powder from it and drops it into the cauldron.

'What the hell did you just do?' the rangur cries, wincing as if someone had thrust a knife in his back and turned it slowly.

'What you should have done already,' Heemal replies calmly. 'That dye you put in the cauldron is for corn yellow. I just darkened it more. We need mustard yellow, remember?' She now looks at her father. The smirk on her face decimates the smugness on his as they stare at each other. Suddenly, the rangur's nostrils flare and his jaw twitches. He can hold it in no longer. He raises his hand and slaps her hard. The rangur has walked into his own trap.

'Get out of here,' he barely manages to say as his lips tremble with the violent spasm that twists his face into an ugly grimace.

Heemal smiles. She starts to leave in triumph. I follow her as I always do, but the rangur stops me. 'Not you. You stay here. It is about time that I have a man by my side.'

Heemal stops at the door and gazes at me. *Come*, her eyes plead, *your place is by my side*. But I remain there, receding away from her with each passing moment like a drowning man from the moon.

7

The Kiss

'It has started to tire,' the rangur says as he scoops up some liquid from the copper cauldron, 'see.'

The liquid he lets drop back into the copper cauldron has turned light green, so light that it almost appears yellow. We had started with dark green, dark as the leaves of an apple tree. 'Get me some more dye,' he says without looking at me. That is how it is between us. Sometimes he speaks to me, sometimes to himself and sometimes, I think, he speaks to someone else who ought to have been there but isn't.

I walk over to the shelves on the wall. I pick up a container. I know this is the one he wants without even opening to see what kind of powder is in it. By now, I know all these containers by heart. I take out a handful.

'No, that is too much. Remember, the yarn has already taken up some shade of green by now. We need only half of what is in your hand. We don't want to overdo it. Too much green and you will be at your wit's end trying to tell it apart from black.'

I close my fist and return almost half the powder from my hand into the container and then hold out the rest for the rangur's approval.

'Yes, that much will do.'

I stand near the cauldron and look at him. He nods and I drop the powder into the boiling water. Today is one of those days when he trusts me with the dye. That is how it is between us. Some days he looks at me and sees a crazy moutt whom he can never trust with anything, with whom he can't even talk properly. And some days he looks at me as if I am someone he has known all his life, or at least someone he ought to have known. Some days he forgets that I am crazy. And some days even I do.

'You must always keep an eye on the liquid. Never let it tire for too long. If you let it tire for too long—' the rangur stops speaking midway, leaving his half-sentence hanging like a noose. He looks at me, his eyes wide open, his mouth agape as if he has woken up from a dream. 'What am I even doing with you!' he says as he shakes his head. He keeps shaking his head as he shifts the yarn over the wooden roller and dips it afresh into the cauldron. The better part of the day is over; this is how the rest of it will be. Silent and sulking.

Dismissed, I get down on my haunches, my knees pressed against my bare stomach inside the fheran. I don't stink as much as I used to. The rangur makes me bathe once a week, more or less. He doesn't want his yarn to stink. It is bad for business, he says.

'What am I even doing with him!' The rangur says again, this time more to himself than to anyone else. I say nothing but just watch: watch him shift the yarn on the roller. Ready to help him if he calls me. But he doesn't. He continues shifting and dipping the yarn all by himself, making sure that all portions of the yarn have soaked up sufficient amounts of the dye.

Hours pass like this.

I am still on my haunches when he cuts out a wet thread from the yarn. He holds it near the hearth to dry it quickly and then checks its colour. He looks satisfied with his work. He takes out the yarn from the cauldron, twists it into a tight knot to wring out as much coloured liquid from it as he can. He wrings it one more time before he hangs it from one of the metal hooks suspended from a wooden beam on the ceiling. He leaves the yarn there to drain the excess liquid dye under its own weight. He is done for the day. He leaves.

It is almost evening now. The curse of Autumn – the days getting shorter and the nights getting colder. Thankfully, I no longer sleep outside under the chinar tree, whose leaves are no longer green but a thousand crimson tongues of a blazing flame. The rangur now lets me sleep here by the smouldering hearth. I get up and lay down near the hearth full of dying, glowing embers. The gasping embers have started to sing their song of evanescence – a warm lullaby that floats and settles over me like a soft, warm blanket – as I watch them grow redder and fainter. Their redness the last resistance of colour against the imminent invasion of the all-vanquishing blackness of the night. As the darkness gathers its forces, the dwindling embers retreat behind my drooping eyelids – melting, flowing; a warm red river making its way through the black unknown, tiring out as the colour fades red, orange, yellow, white; draining, shrinking: two white strands separating into innumerable white threads, cold and supple like a ...

Someone touches my hand and I wake up with a shudder. It is Heemal. She has brought dinner. A bowl of rice with turnips cooked to a mash on top. Rice! By God, we must be rich tonight! I dig in straightaway. From the corner of my eye, I can see the phantasm of Heemal's face made visible by the faint glow emanating from the hearth, as if a dark, snow-clad mountain was lit by a weak, winter sun at dawn. As I keep eating, I gradually feel the sting of her glare. She is usually disgusted I eat food without washing my hands. And she usually highlights her disgust with an angry scowl. But this is not it – this sharp, persistent glare – this is not that usual scowl. Her eyes, two hot pincers trying to peel off my skin, burn with something that is much darker than disgust. It is discomforting, but I keep on eating, not knowing what else to do. The silence around us grows. Heavier. Denser. Each breath adding to its crushing weight. Yet, I refuse to look at her, to face whatever is lurking in her eyes. I keep eating my rice and turnips from the bowl.

And then it explodes, the silence.

'You think you are the son that my father never had?' she blurts out, finally, her voice straining against the reins of her restraint, 'You think you will be the keeper of his secrets, the heir to his craft? That is what you think?'

I say nothing. I just keep on eating.

'But you know what, you are nothing but a donkey to him. A donkey to fetch water for him, hold his roller and open tin containers at his whim. A donkey that costs him what? A fistful of food each day? Could it get any cheaper than that? Can't you see it?'

I finish eating and start to lick my fingers one by

one as if all that mattered in the universe was that lump of rice. After all, that is what should matter to a moutt. In fact, that is the only thing that should matter to a moutt: a belly full of food and a burp to seal it all. I try to play my part as well as I can. I burp. I hear her sigh as she shakes her head.

'You crazy, cruel bastard.' Her voice has grown cold, so cold it could freeze your blood. 'You worship that old fool. Who do you think he is? The god of colours?' She throws her head back and laughs a little. 'God of colours, indeed! The god of red, orange, yellow, green, brown ...' she laughs again, this time a boisterous, full-throated laugh; the peals of her laughter striking like hammer blows in the dark. 'But what about blue? Why is there no blue in your god's kingdom?' she hisses as her laughter morphs into a sneer. 'Why is your puny god scared of blue?' she asks me as she kisses me hard on my lips, her kiss cruel as a poison-tipped dagger.

8

The Stick

Blue? Blue? Blue? Whither the blue? Not in the tin containers by the wall. Nor in the copper cauldron. Not even a stain on the floor where the hanging, dripping yarns always leave a mark. Nowhere to be found, all blue gone like the blue from the winter sky. Even the water in which I stand waist-deep isn't blue any more, only cold. So cold, it could douse hell-fire.

'Dip,' the rangur says.

Dip in the water that isn't blue.

'Take a dip, you filthy rascal. I don't want my yarn to stink.'

Yarns of all colours but blue.

'Take a dip and we will be done for the week.'

A week devoid of blue. As was the week before it. And the week before that ... Week after week of a futile search for blue.

'Take a dip, for God's sake.'

The god of colours is scared of blue. Is he? Is he, really? He brandishes his stick at me, the rangur .

'Do it now, or I swear I will thrash those buttocks of yours till they turn into kebabs.'

Red, red kebabs but whither the blue? Nobody knows. Not the rangur sitting on the steps of the yaarbal. Nor the urchins and idlers who have gathered here for their regular dose of entertainment: a crazy man screaming and swearing at the old dyer while he is forced to bathe. Every week I perform my craziness for all to see. For those who are there and for those who aren't. One can never be too careful. But today, today I am not sure whether I am playing the part or not.

'Blue? Blue? Where is the blue?' I ask my audience at the top of my voice. The only reply I get from them, as expected, is laughter. How else do you respond to the shrieks of a crazy man? 'You bastards, why don't you tell me where the blue is?' I scream and swear as their laughter slides and slithers and coils around my body like a python around its prey. The more I shout, the more it coils around me, stifling me, choking me, crushing me. My lungs are about to burst. I can't breathe ...

I rush out of the water, straight to the rangur sitting on the steps. The stick falls from his startled hand as I grab him by his shoulders. 'Blue? Where is the blue? Tell me, where is the blue? Tell me now.' He has no answers for me, I can see it in his eyes. Only fear and confusion there. Fear and confusion dyed in all colours but blue.

A paroxysm of pain in my right shoulder makes me realize that my audience have stopped laughing and they are, instead, throwing stones at me. They are trying to save the rangur from the wrath of a moutt. And they succeed. I run away. Away from the rangur , away from them all – the whistling urchins and the jeering idlers. Away from the yaarbal. I run into the house. I run into Heemal. I run into the empty pitcher on her hip.

The pitcher is now in smithereens on the floor.

A furious Heemal stares at the pieces and then at me. Her wrath quickly turns into befuddlement as we both realize that I stand naked in front of her. Her eyes – two hungry fawns let loose in a green meadow – roam all over me. They nibble. They graze. They take whatever they want. They trample all over my body, leaving behind trails of hunger and desire. What agony! What sweet ecstasy! She makes me throb and come alive in ways that is a pleasure and torment at the same time. I blush at the thought of what her unabashed gaze is doing to me. And she, in turn, is surprised by my body's uninhibited response to her. Questions start to sprout in her eyes. Questions whose seeds of doubt had been sown from the moment our eyes had met for the first time at the yaarbal. Questions whose answers were always there at the end of her thoughts; all she needed to do was reach out for them. But she never did because she never knew the right questions. And now she does, for the first time, she reaches out for them. She reaches out for answers which render me much more naked than I already am.

'What the hell is wrong with you today?' the rangur shouts, as he barges in with the stick in his hand. 'What was all that about?' Before he could ask me anything else the broken pitcher on the floor catches his attention. 'You broke the pitcher!' he shouts at Heemal. 'Dear Lord, of all the things you could have punished me with, it had to be her! As if it wasn't enough to feed her and clothe her, I must now pay for her carelessness as well! If only I could marry her off and be done with her.'

'Marriage is not the only way to get rid of me,' Heemal replies, her voice sharp as a whiplash. 'There is the whorehouse as well. They will even pay you.'

For a moment, the rangur is too stunned to react. His mouth wide open, he is at a loss for words. Then rage, like wildfire, spreads all over him. You can see the way it makes his face burn. 'You slut! That is what you would like,' the rangur shouts between clenched teeth as the stick in his hand rises high up, like a snake raising its angry head. But before it could strike, before it could come lashing down on Heemal, it finds me in its path, the stick. It has happened on its own – me stepping in to prevent Heemal from any injury. A reflex.

A confused rangur looks at me, as if asking, *What are you even doing?* 'Blue,' I blurt out the only word that comes into my head, 'Blue? Where is the blue? Are you scared of the blue?' I yell as loud as I can.

'Blue! You want blue?' the rangur shouts back. 'You blue son of a blue whore, here, take it,' he says as the stick in his hand comes down on my body with an angry hiss. 'Take as much blue as you want. Here, here, take this. And this. Take it all,' he keeps shouting as the stick in his hand bruises the flesh on my arms, on my shoulders, on my thighs. The assault stops only when his arms go limp with all that angry toil and effort and the stick slips from his hand. A fresh bout of anger makes him shake as he realizes his limp arms will not pick up the stick again; his arms will not help him hit me some more. Helpless, but angry nevertheless, he rushes out.

Heemal picks up the stick and looks at me. 'That was meant for me. All that was meant for me,' she says as she touches the burning flesh on my arms and shoulders. 'Why did you volunteer for it?'

The answer to that would be my confession. But I choose to play the crazy fool once more. '*Tuh,*' I spit on her face, hoping to get back to where we were before all this. Hoping to undo what a brief, foolish moment of passion had undone.

'Don't you think we are past all pretences by now?' she asks calmly as she wipes my spit from her cheek. It is over. I know it. I can feel it in my bones. No more games with her.

'Tell me about blue,' I say as I surrender before her, fully.

9

The Bronze Box

It is said that centuries ago, when our Shah-e-Hamdan, our Amir-e-Kabir, Mir Sayyid Ali Hamdani, blessed be his beloved name, was about to leave from his city of Hamdan, a man came rushing and threw himself at his pious feet. 'O Saint of Saints, for God's sake, take me with you,' he begged. Some said the man was an alchemist who had dabbled in forbidden arts and practices until finally, having realized the error manifest in his doings, he wanted to repent. Others said he was a fugitive from Samarqand, where he had somehow escaped Timur's clutches and now that Timur was almost at the gates of Hamdan, he wanted to escape before it was too late. The whispers and rumours notwithstanding, what Amir-e-Kabir saw at his feet was a fellow human being in need of help. And as was his wont, he didn't turn him away; he gave him his hand. The man kissed it and raised it to his eyes. The vow was taken, the Bayat was made. He was now one of Amir-e-Kabir's disciples. Delighted, the man took out a bronze box from his gown, his only possession, and offered it to Amir-e-Kabir, saying, 'O Murshid of mine, this is all that is left from the labour of my life. Take it and honour me.'

The box was quaint and quite unremarkable in its appearance, except for a faint engraving of what looked like a star on its lid. Although this faint star made Amir-e-Kabir smile, with due grace, he returned the offering without even opening it. Amir-e-Kabir did not need it, the man was told, as he was already blessed by the Almighty with gifts far more wondrous and bountiful. The man had earned the box, so he must keep it. The man smiled and did as he was told. He kissed his murshid's hand once again and joined the other six hundred and ninety-nine disciples of Amir-e-Kabir on their journey to a far-off land.

Now, the disciples of Amir-e-Kabir were holy men who had dedicated their lives to the service of the Almighty and His true path. It was true they need not have bothered themselves with earthly toil and labour, for God Almighty would have provided them sustenance. Yet, they were also men who worked hard and toiled. And with this hard work and toil, they had turned themselves into great artisans and accomplished craftsmen of their time. For it was the creed of Amir-e-Kabir that one must eat only what one earns by the dint of his toil. Thus, they could boast of some of the finest weavers, wood-carvers, calligraphers, bookbinders, metalsmiths, paper-mache artists, etc. amongst themselves. So when a new brother joined them, who was in possession of an artefact that had made Amir-e-Kabir smile, it was but natural that questions would be asked – out of professional curiosity as well as personal.

'I spent my life chasing colours,' he told them as their caravan halted for the night and they gathered around a bonfire after a long, arduous day of travel. 'To be precise, it is the colour blue that I had been after for years. It had all started with an insult. I was betrothed to a girl. Niloufar was her name. As was the custom in our family, I had to get a tunic for her as a pre-wedding gift. With a name like that, the choice of colour of her tunic was all but a foregone decision. I bought the best blue tunic that my dinar could buy and had it sent over to her. A week or so before our marriage day, the tunic was sent back to me with a note that read, 'Pray let it be known which is more resolute: your heart or the colour of your tunic? Would it be a folly to hope your love will not fade away as quickly as the blue of this tunic did?' And the note was not wrong. The tunic that had been as blue as the bluest flower of Niloufar on its day of purchase was now such a pale hue of its former self that one could almost mistake it for an ill-omened white shroud. Furious, I rushed to the draper, but he blamed the dyer. That is but natural, the dyer said when I confronted him. And he went on to explain what a nightmare it was to dye something blue.

'Indigo that is used to dye the fibre blue is the oldest dye and yet the most stubborn. You try to mix it with water, but it remains aloof. No matter how much you coax and coerce it, it refuses to dissolve. You could force it by a long-drawn-out process to somehow give up its colour, but it won't give up its adamancy. You will have a dye solution somehow, but the dye will not penetrate the yarn fibre as all the other dyes do; it will just stick to the fibre's surface like oil on water; the inside – the core of the fibre – will remain untouched. Thus, the yarn will appear to have been dyed blue but it never is truly blue. And what turns it into an embarrassment is that even this semblance of blue wears off over time. The indigo sticking on the surface gets washed off the fibre, revealing the undyed, un-blue core, shade by lighter shade. Almost all dyers sell this inconsistency of blue colour as a marvellous feat. "A living dye," they call it. A dye that changes its hue as if it were sentient, responsive to the changes around it. But in their heart of hearts, they know it is nothing but a fraud. Nothing but their failure and their surrender before the obstinacy of the indigo.

'Full of passionate foolishness, as one is only in his youth, I swore I won't marry till I vanquished this adamancy of indigo and conquered the colour blue once and forever. Only such a victory could reclaim my honour before my betrothed, I declared. And thus passed the years as I lost myself in the alleys and bowels of Samarqand in pursuit of this elusive victory. When the dyers couldn't teach me anything more, I ran to the alchemists. And when the alchemists of the time had nothing more to offer, I turned to the old ones, known and unknown, dead and no more. I ransacked kutub-khane – libraries – and secret dens wherever I could find them, and scoured through texts, sacred and profane. I roamed a world where many a secret unravelled itself before me. And, as animosity is the dowry of secrets, I had my share of enemies. Ironically, the worst of that animosity rose from the most innocuous of those secrets.

'It so happened that one day, an old alchemist teacher came to my door asking for horse chestnuts. I had a large stock of those nuts, as for months I had been trying to work out a new blue dye by mixing the extract of the horse chestnut kernels with indigo powder. The alchemist knew all about it. In fact, it was he who had suggested using kernels in the first place, and he occasionally helped me with the distillation as well. So it didn't surprise me that he had come asking for horse chestnuts at my door. Rather, what surprised me was the fact that he didn't need the kernels; he was asking for the nuts instead. And not just a few or a handful at the most, but for all that I had. The nuts were of no interest to me. Everybody knows you can't eat them; they are not right for the stomach. So what was in it for the alchemist? And what was with this desperation? Even if I refused him, he could easily get them from the bazaar. True, it would take some time to get as much quantity as he was asking for, but what was the rush? I had myself amassed my stock over months, so why couldn't he?

'My interest was piqued and I told him quite emphatically that I wouldn't part with those nuts until he told me what he was up to. It wasn't such a big deal, the alchemist replied, it was just that he needed the nuts to prepare a concoction with which he had been treating a soldier for some time now. This soldier had strength and ambition enough to succeed in the imperial army, but had discovered a particular impediment to his ascension plans. The thing was, every time he lifted a sword to strike at an enemy, his hands would start to tremble violently. By the sheer force of his will, this soldier had trained himself to prevail over any enemy despite the tremors and had even managed to be proficient enough to be made an un-bashi – a rank that put ten soldiers under his command. It was these men under his command that he was afraid his trembling hands would not be able to control. Trembling hands could easily be seen as a sign of cowardice. And nobody wants to serve under a coward. As the young un-bashi had his eyes set on the rank of a yuz-bashi – and maybe even a ming-bashi, one day – the men under his command were only set to increase. The trembling hands would no longer do; he needed a cure.

'Over the course of time, the alchemist had discovered that among the various concoctions that he had prepared for this soldier, it was the fermented distillate of horse chestnuts that gave the best results. It not only calmed down the soldier's hands at the hilt of the sword, but also helped with the blows. They became stronger and swifter. The concoction took away all hesitancy from the hands of the soldier. So successful was the medicine that the soldier was made a yuz-bashi of the imperial forces. Now, as Amir Timur had declared the military expedition to the east, the yuz-bashi expected to be away with the imperial forces for the better part of a year, if not more. He needed the concoction now more than ever. The imperial forces were to leave within a week, so the alchemist needed to prepare the concoction in a quantity sufficient for a year's worth of fighting, and he had just a few days' time to prepare it all. He had little time to waste and he could think of no better and assured source for the nuts than me.

'I gave him the nuts and had forgotten about it all till I came to know about the demise of my alchemist friend almost a year later. Early one morning, the alchemist's head had been found severed from his body. This had come after a night at a tavern, filled with opium fumes and a dozen men whose goading had made the alchemist foolish enough to boast at the top of his voice that it was he who made a sardar – a military leader – out of a young yuz-bashi with the horse chestnuts he had got from me.

'The only thing worse than being a cowardly sardar is being a sardar rumoured to be hiding his cowardice. No doubt the young sardar could not allow such rumours. The alchemist had to be silenced, as had to be everyone who could lend credence to such a rumour. I knew what was coming my way. So, by evening, as the assassins of the imperial sardar arrived at my door, I was already halfway to the city of Hamdan. My days at Samarqand were over once and forever.

'Once in the wondrous city of Hamdan, for the first time in many years, I had nothing to do. There were no scrolls to be read, no chemicals to be distilled, no liquids to be boiled. For the first time in many years, I found myself inside that silent womb of loneliness where you have no one but yourself, where all thoughts like an echo lead only back to you. What was I doing? What was it that I really sought? I searched the folds of my gown and emptied my pockets. There was nothing to show for my years of toil and sweat, except for this brass box that I had managed to take away as soon as I became aware of the danger at my door. Even if this box contained the perfect indigo dye, what good would it do? Niloufar had been married years ago; what would I do with a tunic whose blue would never fade? What colour could be worth a lifetime's pursuit?'

'"*Sibghatallah*!" the answer came from Amir-e-Kabir. His words fell on my ears like a snow-fed waterfall on hot, desiccated rocks. "*Sibghatallah, wa man ahsanu minallah e sibgha* (Colour is from Allah, and who is better than Allah at colouring!)" Amir-e-Kabir recited this verse from Holy Quran as he preached his Friday sermon from the pulpit to hundreds gathered in front of him. Suddenly, the world melted before my eyes and started to reassemble itself in a new way, in a new colour. Then and there I knew I had to follow Amir-e-Kabir, come what may. And here I am, at his beloved feet, and amongst you.'

'And all praise to Allah for that. We welcome you, brother,' the disciples said.

'But what about the bronze box?' one of the more eager ones amongst the disciples – a coppersmith – asked. 'Does it really contain the perfect indigo dye?'

'Maybe,' the man replied with a smile, 'or maybe, it contains something far more wondrous – that is, if it contains anything at all.'

Over the course of the rest of their journey, no matter how many times this story was repeated, it always led to the same question. And the answer, too, was always the same, more or less.

The journey finally came to an end when the caravan crossed over the mountains, on the other side of which a waiting sultan received them with due honour and respect. They had finally reached the vale which, as they had been told beforehand, was as beautiful as if it had germinated from a seed from blessed Paradise. They found that the praise wasn't exaggerated as they spread in ones and twos throughout this vale, carrying the word of the one true God.

But it wasn't just the word of God that spread. What also spread were the new artforms and skills that the disciple–artisans of Amir-e-Kabir had brought over with them. As the new forms of craftsmanship challenged the old, they couldn't prevent being moulded by what they challenged. The alchemy of change was set in motion. The new was moulded into newer, while the old rejuvenated itself. Thus, the vale started to wake up to a new way of life. The old city, in particular, started to bristle with an energy that was foreign in its genius and local in its ingenuity.

As the light spread and the darkness was swept away, it was time for Amir-e-Kabir to leave the vale. But not everyone who had arrived with him went back with him. Some chose to remain behind and some were asked by Shah-e-Hamdan to stay. The man with the brass box was one of the latter. Though he dared not defy his master's wish, the man could not resist pleading, 'O Saint of saints, what shall I do here without you? My place is at your feet, always. Allow me to leave with you. Allow me to follow you wherever you go.'

'You have to stay here,' he was told as the caravan left. 'You belong here. All you need is to find your place.'

Meanwhile, the coppersmith, his fellow traveller who had chosen to stay behind, asked the man with the brass box to join him at his smithy. He needed a helping hand and the brass-box man needed to earn a living, the coppersmith had figured out. They could help each other out. The man agreed. Maybe the smithy was his place. But it wasn't; it was rather a disaster, the man's work at the smithy. He couldn't handle metals no matter how much he tried. It was the same at the perfumist's, the paper-mache artist's, the cap-maker's, the weaver's. Everywhere, it was the same story. The man failed to find his place. And that was how it was till the day he saw the waters of the Jhelum turn blue.

Upstream, someone was overwhelmed by the colours draining out from the yarn she was trying to wash in the river. It was a widow trying to continue her late husband's fast-dwindling trade of dyeing. She was, quite visibly, failing miserably. She was dyeing the Jhelum rather than dyeing the yarn. Then and there, the man knew what he must do. Then and there, he knew he had found his place finally.

The man took the widow as his wife and took up her late husband's trade. He was now a dyer. His years in pursuit of the blue dye had made him as good at dyeing as any professional dyer, if not more. As his trade started to flourish, his old traveller friend, the coppersmith, gifted him a copper cauldron. The copper cauldron had a star inscribed on its neck in commemoration of the star that the man's bronze box bore.

Thus, the man from Samarqand started dyeing yarn by the banks of Jhelum. As years passed by, the widow bore him sons and daughters. The daughters were married off and the sons joined their father in his trade. He taught them everything that he knew about dyeing and colours, except for the colour blue. And when he took to his deathbed, he called aside the son that he deemed worthiest among his offspring, and handed the brass box over to him while whispering something in his ear. Only this son dared to dye anything blue after his father's death. And it was this son who, when he thought his end was nigh, called aside his worthiest son and whispered in his ear while handing over the brass box. And so it kept being passed on – the brass box, the whisper, the ability to dye something blue – from father to worthy son, till it reached my grandfather. Even though my father was the only son my grandfather had, the whisper never reached his ears. As heavens deemed it fit, my grandfather never got the chance to call aside his son. He died when no one, not even he himself, suspected it – in his sleep as he snored unawares.

And to this day, my father cannot decide whether he is unworthy or just unlucky. And though he may act otherwise, deep down he still feels his father did not teach him everything about their trade. He still does not dare to dye anything blue.'

10

The Levy

They are at the door. A pack of them. They always roam in packs, these men from the fort. I know it is them. I don't need to turn and see their faces to know they are from the fort. I know they are. One can always tell when they are around. It is that primeval instinct of survival that makes a prey aware of its predator as it lurks nearby. That stinking concoction of trepidation and revulsion that fills up your guts as fear makes a hostage of your body and disgust at your own cowardice and meek surrender overwhelms you.

'You there,' one of them shouts at me, his voice pickled in bile. 'Come here,' says another one, his voice the same – pickled in bile. 'Quickly,' says another one. 'Quickly. Quickly. Quickly.' Their words creep all over me like a horde of hungry spiders on the hunt. *'RUN.'* Someone screams in my head. 'Run,

run. Run, run. Run, run …' The cry turns into a chant as it falls into a terrible rhythm with the loud, horrible beating of my heart. But I can't. I can't run. I just can't. Petrified, the only thing my body can do is crumble. I dare not move.

'Oye motherfucker, what the hell are you doing standing there like that? Are you an idiot or what?' says one of them.

A trembling silence is the only answer I can muster as a dry, swollen tongue sinks under its own weight to seal off the cave of my throat, stifling the words within.

'Show us your face. And show it now lest you regret having a face for the rest of your wretched life,' says another.

My legs start to tremble as warm, rancid liquid cascades down my cold, coarse thighs, collecting in a dirty yellow puddle between my feet.

'Son of a bitch! Is that piss?' says one of them.

'Did you just piss yourself?' says another.

'But we are just beginning to get to know each other, aren't we?'

'Leave him alone,' Heemal shouts as she rushes past me.

'Now, now, now! What do we have here?' says one of them.

'She is a feisty one, this one is!' says another.

'Girl, step aside. You don't want to get caught up in all this. We are on imperial duty. Do you know what the punishment is for interrupting imperial work?'

Heemal's angry answer to that, the rangur realizes from inside the house, could be fraught with danger. So he leaves his cauldron and throws himself at the feet of one of them before Heemal can open her mouth again. 'Mercy, huzoor, mercy! She is a little hot-headed but she means no impudence, huzoor. She only spoke for this moutt, this crazy one, out of pity.'

'Let go, you son of a bitch!' shouts the man at whose feet the rangur lays prostrate. 'You have ruined my trousers, you filthy faggot!' he shouts as he kicks away the rangur . In his rush, the rangur had forgotten the red dye on his hands. And as he grovels at the man's feet, his hands, like the bloody paws of a terrified animal, leave their marks on his trousers.

'Hell be my everlasting abode!' the rangur cries slapping his forehead, his fingers leaving red imprints all over it as well. 'I am a bastard with hooves and horns, that is what I am. Forgive me, huzoor, forgive me for His Majesty's high sake and your majesty's little sake as well. I will get those stains washed off in no time, I promise you that. I swear on the graves of all the saints, I will do that. Let me just take your trousers off ...'

'Don't you dare touch our clothes again,' says one of them.

'Of course, of course. I won't, I won't. Your wish is our command, huzoor. Whatever you say, huzoor, whatever you say.'

'You will have to pay for a new set of trousers,' says another one.

'Huzoor!' The rangur cries as he gulps down his spit in dismay.

'Should we drag you to the fort then?' says another.

'Mercy! Mercy! I will pay, huzoor. I will. I will.'

'Of course you will, whatever were you thinking? Now that leaves only the matter of the levy on this crazy one over here.'

'Levy on the moutt? What in God's name is that?' the rangur cries out angrily despite knowing better.

'You have to pay for the moutt,' says one of them.

'It is the law,' says another.

'All unclaimed things belong to the Crown.'

'Indeed, huzoor, indeed. But then it is the Crown that should be paying me, huzoor. Shouldn't it?' The rangur replies as he somehow gets his voice under control. 'The Crown should pay me for feeding and housing this unclaimed one and keeping his bones warm. He is all trouble and expense, huzoor. I just took pity on him thinking God Almighty may take pity on my sinful soul on the Day of Judgement. Is pity to be taxed, huzoor?'

'Hold your tongue, you wily bastard. What do you take us for – idiots?' says one of them.

'The levy is not for your so-called pity but it is for the labour that you have been enjoying for free,' says another.

'Yes, yes, free labour. Did you think we would not come to know how you make him labour like a donkey every day? Do you deny that he slaves away at your cauldrons every day? You think you can abuse imperial property like that?' says another.

'Or should we consider this plundering imperial property? Do you even know what the punishment is for theft of imperial property?'

The rangur once again falls at one of the men's feet, but this time he is careful not to touch his trousers or feet. 'Huzoor, may my seven generations be sacrificed at your auspicious feet. I am but a poor man. I don't know the law. I don't know anything. I am a wretched ignoramus with sheep intestines for brains. If I have erred in front of the law, consider it a blind man's trespass. Forgive me, please. Forgive me as you would forgive a thirsty ant that falls into the imperial well.'

'He is asking for forgiveness?' says one of them.

'Let us be merciful,' says another.

'But mercy, like his pity, does not and will not come free.'

The rangur empties his pockets and empties every nook and cranny of his house that was supposed to safekeep money or anything valuable, and offers it all to the pack at his door. But it isn't enough. It never is.

'Is your life worth only this much?' says one of them.

'Huzoor, I swear upon my soul this is all I have. If you find even a single dime left on my person or anywhere in my house, I will forfeit my life.'

'You cannot forfeit what you have forfeited already,' says another.

'Be that as it may, if he is so hell-bent on serving the Crown as a corvee labour, then off to begaer he must go, who are we to object? We are sending a fresh lot tomorrow to the frontier. Let him join them.'

The rangur turns pale as he realizes the game of words is over. There is to be no more masquerading of words as pleas and bargains. Everything becomes meaningless before the threat of the begaer. Everything else becomes meaningless when it comes to survival. Even the pomposity of his speech beats a retreat before the imminent threat, leaving behind only the naked, helpless words of despair. 'I will pay whatever you say. Just give me time to get it from somewhere. Believe me, I don't have anything else left in the house,' the rangur says with a voice bereft of all signs of life, the words so weak in his mouth as if someone had sucked all the blood out of his tongue.

'What is to be done now?' says one of them.

'If only we could help!' says another.

'Maybe we could. If it is money that he needs, there is this very nice moneylender that we know. We can vouch for this man if he wants. Do you want us to?'

The rangur nods his willingness.

'And you,' says one of them to Heemal as they are about to leave, 'You better learn to keep that tongue in check.'

'Learn some manners from your father,' says another.

'There won't be any leniency next time,' says the last of them as they take the rangur with them.

'You know what that means?' Heemal asks me as soon as they are gone. Her voice on the verge of breaking, on the verge of falling down a precipice. To such depths, to such horrible depths of despair. No, no, not now. Not now ...

'You know what that means?' Heemal asks again but her words lose their way in the catacombs of my ears as I try to outrun the inevitability that is the answer to her question. But can I?

'You must leave,' the words are spoken. The question is answered. The sentence pronounced. There is nothing that she or I can do about it. We both know it. We both knew it as soon as the pack had arrived at the door. Leave, I must. That much is inevitable. But like this? Just like this?

Yes, like this. I must leave just like this. Just like death. One ordinary moment – just any ordinary moment – it is all over. You have to leave. You must leave.

You leave.

11

The First Knot

'Is that it?' Abli Bab asks me in his cave. *Is this it,* I ask myself as I look at the bronze box in my hand. *This is it,* Heemal had said at the door, *this is where we part. This is all I can offer before you leave. Take it,* she had said, *take this box and may it lead you to what you seek.* That was it and she was gone.

'Is that really it?' Abli Bab repeats as I close my eyes and try to hold on to the face that had turned away from me at the door. A face that, like a ripple on a lake, is in a hurry to extinguish itself. No matter how hard you try, you cannot keep it together; you cannot hold on to it. Its existence is nothing more than a perpetual dissipation …

'But … how! ... Where? ...' Abli Bab fumbles his words as his voice hits the crescendo of incredulity. He cannot take his eyes off the box in my hands. Slowly but greedily, he reaches out for it as if it was the forbidden fruit that I held in my hands. A shiver runs through his body as his fingers trace the faint star inscribed on the lid of the box. 'By all that is holy and profane, this is incredible! Simply incredible! I can't believe it! You found it? Just like that? Are you really holding it in your hands?'

I am. I really am. *Take it,* she had said, *this is all that I can offer.* And she offered it to me. And I took it. And now she is gone. Really gone. All that I am left with is this box. And it gets heavier every time I try to recall her face, this box. Heavier and heavier. Way too heavy. I drop the bronze box into the eager, outstretched hands of Abli Bab.

'Incredible! Simply incredible!' he grins as he turns the bronze box in his hands. 'Time to open it up,' he whispers once he has had his fill of the exterior. He pries open the lid. The box is filled with blue powder. So blue as if someone had ground a piece of the summer sky to dust. Abli Bab pinches some from the box. 'What is this?' He asks me as he rubs the grains between his fingers. It leaves a vivid blue stain on the tips of his fingers.

'This is dye powder, right?' he says as he tries to wipe clean his fingers on his fheran sleeve. It doesn't work, the tips of his finger remain obstinately blue. He tries to lick them clean but he just ends up with a blue stain on his tongue as well.

'Pretty strong stuff, I must say. It doesn't let go of you,' he says as he keeps trying to wipe away the blue from his fingers. But he cannot, no matter how much he tries, the tips of his fingers remain obstinately blue. 'You did it, you crazy idiot!' Abli Bab suddenly cries, waving his fist as he gives up on getting his fingers clean of the blue stain. 'You lucky bastard! It takes men a lifetime to find something like this – if they find something at all, that is. But here you are.'

Yes, here I am. Here I am amidst this desolation of fulfilment, adrift still sands of stupefaction. Alone, alone, my God, how alone I am under this sky that has lost its bearings!

'Now, this has to remain between us. You understand that, right? This has to remain within this cave. I will get you whatever you need. You must begin right away,' Abli Bab says.

Begin right away, how does one do that? Where does one begin? From the first knot? Yes, maybe. Tie that first knot. And then the next. And then another. And another …

I must begin anew, one knot at a time.

12

The Cave within the Cave

Blue warp. Blue weft. And only blue threads to tie them all. Knot after blue knot, I tie. As many as I can. However I can. There is no taalim to be followed, no instructions to be obeyed. It is just knot after blue knot to be tied. However I can, as many as I can ...

How long will it take? I do not know. How long has it already been? I do not know. Time in this cold, dark cave has been reduced to a bright pendant hanging precariously from a crevice up there somewhere, as light – sunlight, moonlight – finds and loses its way through this crevice in the roof at its own whim, the oscillation between its appearance and disappearance as irregular as a dying man's breath. Even if the light were to find its way in here – regularly, punctually – through that crevice, it still would not matter. For there are days when nothing matters – light, darkness; blue, red; hunger, thirst; sleep, fatigue – nothing whatsoever matters except for this maddening, hysterical rush to tie the knots on the loom. As many as I can, however I can. On such days, I can feel the wind under my carpet, I can almost touch the clouds. On such days, I fly.

Time, on such days, tiptoes into oblivion outside this cave.

And then there are days when nothing matters, again. Nothing whatsoever. Not even the knots. Especially not the knots. What does it matter whether the knots are tied or not? In the vacuous emptiness of the universe, what folly it is to knot something into being and leave it to the mercy of the cruel meaninglessness. What idiocy it is to assume that a knot – any knot – in this godforsaken cave could be of significance when the only language of a sky full of stars is insignificance. On such days, I hate it all – the loom, the knots, the weaving. What foolishness! What idiocy! What a gratuitous waste of labour and toil! Time, on such days, is a rack that stretches you across eternity.

Time thus waxes and wanes in this cave like a shadow on the wall, while I am chained to my loom, forced to watch it all.

'Is it done then?' Abli Bab says as he squeezes into the cave. He has arrived, as he does every now and then, with food and words. 'Is it done?' he asks again as he points to the carpet on the loom.

No! No, it isn't! It is not done yet. It cannot be. It should not be. There are a thousand more knots to be tied, a thousand times thousand at least. There must be. There ought to be. There has to be. Shouldn't there be? A knot after knot after knot after knot … till … till … till what? I don't have a wusteh to tell me that this is it, the last knot is tied, we are done. Even if he were here, would it have made any difference? This cave is no karkhan. There is no tyranny of the taalim here. The wusteh in here, shorn of all his authority, is just a weaver. Just like any other weaver. And any wusteh reduced to a weaver would tell you that you can tie a knot after knot till the trumpet of Judgement Day is blown and you still would not be done. The weaver thinks it is the taalim that tells the wusteh when to stop, but the wusteh knows the taalim is just an excuse to stop. What then should be my excuse to stop? Something as arbitrary as the silence of the taalim?

Yes, why not?

Something as abrupt.

Yes, yes.

Arbitrary and abrupt.

Any day.

Anytime.

Today.

Tonight.

Why not?

Tonight. Yes … Yes … Tonight …

'Tonight, I will finish it.'

My words jerk Abli Bab into rapt attention, as if lightning had passed through his veins. 'Tonight?' he says as he reconsiders the carpet on the loom with renewed interest. 'Very well then, you know where to find me. I will be waiting up there.'

13

Snow and Fire

A brief moist moment of lightness, that is how it feels on my hand. As if a butterfly had kissed my hand. I look up. There is more. On my cheeks, on my forehead, on my nose, on my lips. They are falling like feathers from the sky, the snowflakes. Listless, they float and drift in the air, unsure where to go. As if they could go anywhere else but down! As if they could defy their downfall. I shake my head at their frivolity and keep climbing up Haer Parbat.

It is not as dark as it ought to be. Maybe it is the snow. It has somehow diluted this moonless, starless night. Or maybe it is one of those nights when darkness refuses to hide you. But there is no turning back now. I keep climbing up.

Within no time, the vagrant, languid descent of the reluctant snowflakes transforms into determined, rigorous snowfall. As the flakes turn colder and heavier, every voice, every sound is muffled. The silence of the night is amplified and it grows and grows. Till it turns into a white void. The demons in my head rush in to fill this void with their screams and shrieks. All my fears have a voice now. *Go back*, they shout. *You shouldn't be here*, they say in my wusteh's voice. In the rangur's voice. In Abli Bab's voice. In my own voice. *Turn back, there is still time. Creep back to your cave.* They laugh. *Look at you. Just look at you.* The laughter redoubles. *If only you could look at yourself.* I close my eyes to do the same, to look at myself, but all I can see is Heemal's face. *Thu*, she spits on my face. *Didn't I give you this*, she says with a bronze box in her hand. The bronze box with the star. *I gave this to you. To you, you understand. To you …*

'There you are!' Abli Bab almost screams as he sees me. I have reached the ledge of Haer Parbat near the shrine. Abli Bab has been waiting for me. He has been for a while, the footmarks on the faint layer of snow on the ground show he has been pacing around.

'This snow, I tell you! I thought you would not come tonight. But then it is better this way. You see, snow keeps them tucked in,' he says with a sly smile as he points towards the fort above with his eyes, 'Blinds them as well.' He tries to sound calm but the rambling betrays his composure, as does the restless fidgeting of his thumbless hands. He looks at me, expecting me to say something, to take charge and relieve him of his restlessness. But I say nothing. I have nothing to say. I just stand here, quiet as a shadow.

Snow is falling in lumps now. It has started to gather on the ground. Its indifference exaggerates the coldness of my response to Abli Bab. Overwhelmed, he throws his hands up in the air only to bring them back to his hips as he realizes the only thing that the sky has to offer him is the snow – cold and fleeting. He sighs. There is no other way but to get it done. 'Well then, have you brought it?' he asks me as he resigns himself to the inevitability of it all.

I nod as I pat the blue carpet rolled into a tight bundle under my arm. My hand lingers on the carpet as it feels warm somehow. Warm and throbbing. I can feel the warmth seeping in through my fingers and sending ripples of pleasure throughout me. The ripples swell and rise and rapidly turn into waves. A shiver runs through my body as beads of sweat break out on my nape. Abli Bab can sense the fire within me. The flames have reached him as well. The weight of restlessness is off his shoulders as his arms droop to his sides. 'What now?' he says with a smile, his voice no longer taut as silk stretched on a loom.

I return his smile. 'There is only one thing to do,' I say as I find my voice for the first time tonight. They delight me – my words and my voice. They brim with the energy of a crackling fire that is about to claim a forest.

'Come on then. What are we waiting for?'

We both walk to the edge of the ledge. The fire within me is raging now. It spreads to my arms, to my hands as I hold tightly the rolled blue carpet in my hands. With a single, swift motion, like a fisherman throwing his net, I unfurl the carpet and let it go at the same time. For a moment, the blue carpet holds its shape. For a moment, the carpet floats as it struggles to balance itself against the air. For a moment, every knot, every fibre of the carpet comes alive. For a moment, the carpet is all that I had wanted it to be. A blue pile of knots unfurling all of its glory as it proclaims its own miracle. The pangs of its birth undermined and overwhelmed by its mere existence.

For a moment, I stand here as sanctified as any mother at childbirth.

For a moment – a brief, light moment – the carpet flies.

And then … then … Then it is gone. It is all gone. The moment is lost. The carpet is gone. Its bony tassels, like helpless tiny hands, flailing all the way down as they desperately try to hold on to the broken ropes of the falling snow.

14

The Ashes

A cold, smouldering sky, its ashes falling with an unbearable lightness. Piling up, these ashes – these inchoate seeds of an inconsolable loss – sprout into a white wilderness all around. A shivering, silent shroud stretching itself over everything, everywhere; reducing everything everywhere to a pale, cold desolation. Acres and acres of frozen disquiet wherever your eyes turn to. No respite from it anywhere. Sharp-beaked birds of unease rise from these white, frigid fields of sorrow and come flying to peck at me. Again and again. Flock after sharp, silent flock. Such grief, such pain! As if my heart were broken into a thousand pieces and each piece mounted on a frozen lance.

It has been snowing thus for days now. For days now, that blue carpet keeps falling down Haer Parbat, its tassels flailing, crying for help all the way down.

Again and again that moment of devastation repeats itself. The echoes of the downfall setting a vortex in motion in my head:

What should have been done? What could have been done? What should have been done? What could have been done? What should have been done? What could have been done?

'You have no one to blame,' Abli Bab says as he sucks furiously on his jajeer. He refuses to look me in the eye. 'The choice was always yours, remember?'

Yes, yes, I remember that illusion you called choice. I remember it all too well. Yes, indeed, the choice was made. The price was paid. Yet, somewhere at the foot of this Hill of Sparrow – this hill of sorrow – my carpet lies buried under a mound of snow. A mound that keeps growing. Growing and growing and turning into a parbat. A hillock. The Hillock of Ashes. Its weight unbearable. The helplessness insufferable. Must the carpet be left there to be crushed underneath it all forever?

Running, tumbling, sliding, struggling, I rush to the foot of Haer Parbat. I dig through the snow with my bare hands. Here, there, everywhere. But who has ever undone a burial? Who has ever unmade the ashes? I keep on digging. I keep on trying till the cold makes my fingers revolt. They are beyond me now, these fingers of mine. I can feel them no more. My hands give up. I give up. Why rake up the ashes? Why disturb the dead? Why undo a burial? It isn't too bad, after all, to be buried under the snow. A stillborn sleep in a white, inconscious womb. The stillness of blood so absolute that no thought can perturb it, no memory can disturb it. Not even a dream to delude it. How tempting it is – this indifference to the vagaries of blood and thought, this liberation from the servitude of the senses. How tempting it is to just stand here and let the snow swallow you like a toothless, tongueless mouth, and inter you forever in its comatose belly of white oblivion ...

'What are you doing?' Abli Bab comes calling. 'For God's sake, why are you out here? What if someone sees you? What foolishness is this? What craziness is upon you?' He looks down at me, angry impatience spread all over his face. 'You will be the ruin of us all,' he shakes his head as he speaks. 'Come,' he says as he struggles to keep his voice down, 'Let us go back before it is too late.'

'Go back,' I roll the words slowly on my tongue. They taste like ashes. 'Go back where?' I spit out the words.

'What do you mean, go back where? Up there, where else? Enough with this horse-show. Come on, let us get going.'

The certitude with which he says those words, the disdain with which he turns away and starts to plough his way through the snow, confident that I will follow him, disgusts me.

'No. I am not going back there.'

'What? Not going back? Where else is left there for you to go?'

Snow crackles under my feet like broken eggshells as I walk away from Abli Bab. And it keeps crackling under my feet as I walk across a sea of eggshells, as I walk away from Haer Parbat. Away from the vertigo of that cold cave. Away from the web of those endless knots. Away from everything, I step into the desert of ashes. I walk over desolate dunes of snow and sorrow. I walk and walk without meaning to go anywhere. But my feet have a memory of their own. Like a pair of desert birds, they know a way past all desolation. Step by step they follow an old, familiar path. A path that ends at a door.

A dark, brooding door.

Cold and spent, I stand before this door like a heap of ashes. The door opens. A shadow flits. A face appears. A startled Heemal stares back at me. Her mouth wide open as if to scream, but no sound comes out of it – as if her mouth were full of ashes.

15

Mothers and Daughters

'Why did you come back?' The pain in Heemal's voice is much worse than the pain in my fingers as warmth returns to them from the fire kindled in the hearth, that old hearth. The ache only gets stronger as the chilblains on my hands and feet start to thaw.

'Why did you?' Heemal keeps asking as she dumps a coarse woollen blanket over my shoulders. It isn't enough, she realizes. Cold that has seeped into and now nestles in the marrow of my bones won't be coaxed out so easily. She brings another blanket – or maybe it is an old rug – and puts it over me. The pain in my fingers and toes reaches an unbearable, excruciating peak before it starts to ease off gradually. Heemal sees the change as the violent redness of my swollen fingertips starts to fade. Assured that there is nothing more that needs to be done immediately, she sits by my side, beside the hearth.

'They took Father away,' her voice trails off as she looks away from me. 'They took Father away,' she repeats after a few moments of silence; her voice this time comes from a far-off place, as if she were crying for help from the bottom of a deep, dried-up well. 'They came looking for you. They came looking for you again and again. And Father had to pay them every time. And then when Father could not pay anything anymore, they grabbed him and took him away. They still keep coming, every now and then. They threaten to send Father away to the frontier unless something is done.' She is no longer speaking to me. Her words have carried her away, carried her to that wasteland where words starve into silence. It frightens me, this quagmire of silence that she is sinking in. In a desperate bid to hold on to her, I say the only thing that may reach her, the only thing that she may wish to hear. 'We will bring him back. Don't worry. We will.'

There is no truth in that, I know. Her father is gone. There is no coming back from them. Nobody ever does. Even she must know it for the lie that my assurance is. Yet, somehow, she looks at me with such tenderness, with such hope, that I want to believe my own lie.

'You shouldn't have come back,' she says with a sob. I don't know what to do except to take her hand in my hands. She stiffens at my touch.

'Oh God, your hands are still so cold!' she scolds me with the affected anger of a mother whose child has hurt himself.

'Get me something warm to drink then,' I say with a smile. But my words seem to stun her. Mouth wide open, she seems to have swallowed her tongue. Two large teardrops roll down her perturbed cheeks in a hurry. It takes a few moments before she finally finds words to speak. 'Something to drink ... Yes ... Yes, something to drink ... Yes, yes, of course. Let me go get you something to drink.'

She takes her time.

When she finally returns, there is an earthen cup in her hands, warm, enticing vapours rising from it like a siren's song. She walks up to me, but does not hand me the cup. She holds on to it as she sits by my side. She raises the cup as if to drink from it herself. 'Do you know the story of Rustam the Mighty's birth?' she asks me as she changes her mind at the last minute and hands the cup over to me. I take a sip. The warmth that spreads in my mouth is irresistible. I gulp the rest of it in one go. As the hot liquid makes its way down my throat, it leaves behind a trail of warmth all the way down to my gut. The warmth settles in the pit of my stomach like a plump cat curled into a tepid ball of fur.

'It is said when Rustam's mother Rudaba the Glowing One was at the end of her term, she could not bring Rustam forth. No matter how much she laboured, no matter how hard she pushed, she just could not bring her child into this world. It was then that her husband Zaal the White-Haired began to fear for his unborn son and, some say, for his wife.'

The cat in my stomach stretches itself and its warm fur starts to spread like fog. It grows bigger and warmer, filling up my limbs, rising up into my chest. Its languorous breath warming every organ of my body. Slowly and softly, it makes its way into my head.

'At the height of his desperation, Zaal the White-Haired remembered the feather of Simurgh that was in his possession. A parting gift from that great bird who had nursed and raised Zaal when he had been abandoned on the Alborz Mountains. Zaal fetched the feather and threw it on the sacred fire. Lo and behold! The mighty Simurgh stood before him in all her shining glory. "O great Simurgh, help my dying child as you once helped another child – me," Zaal the White-Haired begged.'

The fog rises into my head. It is getting warmer and heavier up there. Dizzier. I can't seem to stand still. My head keeps dropping. Heemal comes to my rescue. She makes me lie on the floor and places my head in her lap.

'Of course, Simurgh could not refuse her son. She came up with a solution. She made Zaal brew an ancient drink. A warm, soothing drink.'

The feline fog now presses on my eyelids with its tepid, furry paws. I can no longer keep my eyes open. I try to fight those strong, heavy paws, but Heemal's fingers running through my hair drain all my remaining strength.

'A warm soothing drink to put Rudaba to sleep. A sleep deep enough for her belly to be cut open to bring out Rustam. A sleep deep enough to save someone.'

My eyes fall shut, but deep down somewhere I am wide awake. I can feel Heemal's moist lips on my brow. I can hear her ugly sobs and broken wails. But no matter how much I try, I can't see her face.

16

Wheezes and Darkness

Nothing but darkness – that is all you will find in here, my son. Darkness and, of course, my wheezes, that is all that fills this prison, or cell, or whatever you may like to call it. Me, I like to call it a pit, you see. A grave, sort of, you know, but no angels visit you here, even if only to question you. But no sir, nobody comes. That is why it is a pit, not a grave. You see, the grave has its angels and torturers, but the pit, well, it does not. Not any that I know of so far. Darkness and wheezes are all there is in here, you see. And sometimes, when I am in the mood, there are my words as well. Who listens to my words if nobody comes here, you ask? True, true. Sometimes – almost all the time, to be fair – there is actually nobody here to listen to them. But then it doesn't matter, you see. Why should it? It doesn't matter to me. That is it. And since it doesn't matter to me, it does not matter whether they do to anyone else. You see. Maybe you don't. But like I said, it doesn't matter. Why do

I keep speaking then, you ask? Well, you see, words are like the wind you must get them out; otherwise, they bloat you up from inside and nobody wants to die by exploding for no reason, he he he … Anyway, back to the point at hand, anybody listening or not – that should never bother you. Come to think of it, nothing bothers me anymore! Even this darkness, even this doesn't bother me. Not that it could have anyway. I am blind you see. So, eyes open, eyes shut – it is all the same to me. But you, my dear, well, darkness must suck at your eyes like leeches. Darkness, you see, it feeds on light. These leeches will keep on sucking at your eyes till they make sure they have sucked out all the memory of light from there. Slurrrppppp … Greedy little things these vulgar little leeches, I tell you. Nothing ever satiates them, not even that last drop of light in your eyes. Always looking for more. There is no escaping them, you see. There is no escape from here, dear. Absolutely none. There isn't even if you were to volunteer for the begaer. Imagine someone volunteering for the begaer! Ha ha ha … Would you have ever believed that someone would volunteer for begaer? Yet here we are. If only we could, wouldn't we beg them to take us for begaer? Anything anywhere but out of here, right? Anything anywhere but out there in the light. But no, sir, there is to be no begaer for us. Only darkness and wheezes. Ha ha ha ha … Begaer, you see, is for people who they know what to do with. The people they understand and know how to use. But people like us, who they don't know what to do with, we are never called for anything. They just dump us here. In this pit or grave – call it whatever you like; it doesn't matter, you see. It is all darkness and wheezing in here. And this is where they leave us – in darkness and wheezes. Left here and forgotten. How long have I been forgotten? I don't know. You see, I don't even remember why I was forgotten in the first place. Don't be surprised. Nothing much there. You see, my dear, history is full of blind old men like me who forget their past, can't see their present but have memories of the future. Yes, yes, I do have memories of the future. I can see the future, is that what I should say? No, but that is not what I am saying. What I am saying is that I have memories of the future, yes, memories of the future; it is not the same thing as seeing the future, you see. How do I explain that? Well, frankly, I cannot. But then, there is no harm in trying, is there now? It isn't as if we have anything better left to do here. It is either that, or darkness and wheezes. The choice is easy, no? Hmmm … so let me see. How do I explain it? Errr … well … you see … it is like this … like, you know … It is not like I close my eyes and I see the future … It is not like I see something there unfolding and unveiling itself … like somebody doing something … Or like what is going to happen with this one or that one … or what is going to happen to this place or that … it is not like I have a vision waiting for me every time I close my eyes. No sir, it doesn't work that way. It is just that sometimes it just comes to me, you see, what is going to happen with someone or how things will turn up somewhere. It just comes to me as if I had known it all along, only I had forgotten about it. As if something or someone made me remember it, you see. Like a memory ... Only these are the memories of things that are yet to happen ... The memories of the future ... That is how it is ... you understand that? I hope you do. There isn't anything else that I can do about it otherwise. You must go with me on this one. You better do so because there isn't much you can do about it either. You see, you are stuck in here with me like a mother buried with a foetus in her pregnant womb. Was that also one of the memories? The pregnant woman in her grave? How do I know? Maybe, maybe not. You see, I don't like to meddle with the other world and I like to draw a line with my memories at the grave. No peeking behind that. There are certain things that are not supposed to be meddled with, you see. And God Almighty, I beseech your forgiveness if I or any of my memories ever have inadvertently done anything of that sort. You should never gamble with your afterlife, mind you. It isn't worth it. Besides, there is no coming back from there, he he he ... Maybe it is an actual memory then? Well, again, I don't know. How is one supposed to distinguish between the past and the future when you know nothing of either? Now, now, let us not go into that. It is a proper rabbit hole, that one. And I had hoped to avoid it. Shouldn't have brought it up. It complicates everything and does no good to anyone, you see. But then, as I said, words are like the wind; you cannot keep them in, particularly when you need so badly to keep them in. Trrrrr … they slip out just like that despite all the efforts you make to keep your trap shut tight. Trrrrr and it is all out, you see. A fart and no more. God, that is another rabbit hole there – words and the wind. There is no coming back once you go down that one. And now is not the time for that. Let us get back to where we were. Now where were we? Darkness and wheezes. Memories of the future. Ah yes! Memories of the future, you see. Why then am I in here, you ask? I should be out there. I could be their greatest weapon. Greater than even fear. To be honest, that is what I think too. You see, what couldn't I do for them? Catch their foes before they actually turn into foes, take the surprise out of any surprise attack, find the places where lost cats are eventually going to turn up … just a few things off the top of my head, you see. And imagine what else I could do in the service of someone who already reigns over the present and the past. Imagine how I could help him extend his dominion of tyranny to the future as well. Imagine that! History certainly hasn't seen one of those, has it? None that I know of, at least. Why then am I here, you ask? Beats me, if I may be allowed to say so plainly. I do have a theory, though. In fact, it is just a theory, mind you. But, you see, we will have to make do with it till I or you or anyone else finds something better. Although I doubt anyone else will. So it must do. Remember, we are stuck here. Mother and child in a grave. Or in a pit. Whatever works for you. Anyway, here it goes.

The bards sing of a blind man like me in the Yunnan of old. Nothing much there, you see. As I told you already, history is full of men like me – old and blind – who have memories of the future. Now, when the Queen bore a son to the King of Yunnan, this old blind man remembered or foresaw – whatever works for you – that this newborn baby would grow up to kill his father and bed his mother. The king, you see, as any king would have done in his place, decreed that the baby must be done away with. For the greater good, that is. I don't judge him. Even a non-king would have done the same, even without the additional responsibility of the greater good on his shoulders. Now, he was a kind man, this King of Yunnan. He couldn't let it all happen in front of his own eyes. So, he asked his swordsman to do it – this act – at some faraway place, away from his royal weeping eyes. The swordsman, you see, happened to be a shepherd in his free time. So he knew of this nice glen in the mountainside forest which marked the border of the kingdom, where he used to take his sheep for grazing every now and then. But once he reached the glen, this shepherd–swordsman found himself unable to do it, unable to cut off the head of this thumb-sucking sad newborn who kept staring at him as if asking for milk. Unfortunately, the shepherd–swordsman too had a kind heart. Like king like people, as the saying goes. Even if I don't do it, this baby will die anyway, he told himself. The forest is an unforgiving place, as are the wolves out there. Forever hungry and cruel. All he needed to do was to leave the child there and run as far away as he could from the mewls and cries. And, you see, that is what he did. And that is what you get when you employ shepherds as swordsmen. Too much kindness for anyone's good. The thing with kindness, you see, is that kindness is a bitch. It comes to bite you in your arse when you are looking away. I like to think that the shepherd–swordsman would have been put to his own sword as soon as he returned to the palace. That would have been nice and proper. Besides, it would have meant that the king would never have to look at the face of his child murderer. Although the bard doesn't sing of that. The bard rather sings of how the newborn didn't die. How some passers-by – probably thieving wood-cutters from the neighbouring kingdom or some shepherds from the other side, whatever works for you – found this baby and took him to their own childless king. Here was the answer to the pleas and prayers of the royal couple. No doubt about that. I like to think that those wood-cutters or shepherds were also put to the sword as soon as they handed over the baby to the king. No loose ends, you see. That is what a proper tale should always take care of, its loose ends. Besides, no king likes intermediaries between himself and God except clerical ones. No king particularly likes the gossiping common kind who cannot be trusted with state secrets, who in a drunken stupor might boast of God's gift that they brought to the king from the mountainside. Kindness, remember, is a bitch out there to bite you in the arse. Anyway, the boy grows into a man and the future foretold comes to haunt him again. Someone, some old blind man probably – although the bard says it was a woman but, you see, I don't believe him. It has to be an old blind man, probably wheezing too, while we are at it. No loose ends, as I told you already. So, this someone told the young man that he would end up killing his father and bedding his mother. What could the young man do? Hang himself, you say? But that takes courage. And would it have made for a good tale if he had? No? That is what I thought. So, the young man does not hang himself; instead, he runs away from his adopted parents. Away to some other kingdom where he could never come across his father or mother to kill or to bed, intentionally or accidentally. He quarrels with the first man he comes across in this new land. After all, you see, what better way to vent one's frustration than to lash out at a stranger? One word led to another. One thing led to another. And the young man ended up killing the stranger. From there, the bard sings, the angry young man went further on to defeat some monster or something of the sort that had plagued the kingdom which the young man had ended up in. You see, killing a monster becomes much easier once you kill a man. It is basically the same thing, only one out of the two takes greater effort. Anyway, no sooner had this monster been defeated than this young man was made the king of the land. For the land was kingless. Their king had been found dead quite recently. The young man was a godsend. He had proved his credentials by rescuing the land from the curse of that monster. So it was decided that he should be crowned the king. Kindness, you see, it always pays you back as soon as it has the opportunity. Once he took the throne, it was but quite natural that he should take up the late king's bed as well. No loose ends, you see. So he took the Queen for his wife. Now I don't know whether you saw it all along or not, but let me tell you that the stranger this young man had killed was the king that this land originally had. In fact, he was that same king who had ordered the death of his child not so long ago before the shepherd–swordsman had messed it all up. There you go! The future foretold is fulfilled! As I said, you should always take care of loose ends. So, it all ended up as the old blind man had told it would. A sad story, you say. Yes, sad indeed. But then that is history and song. All sadness. And foolishness. They keep on repeating the tune and we just keep on dancing like monkeys at the fair, you see. What has all this got to do with me? Well, you see, what do you make of this story? The Moving Finger writes, and having writ, moves on. That is what you say. Yes, yes, of course that old drunkard of Nishapur had it right. But this is not it. There is more here than just moving fingers and wrists. You see, if it had not been so, then there is no reason for me to be here. I should be out there, with them, telling them what the Moving Finger wrote before the finger moves on. But I am not. I am here. It doesn't add up. How do you solve this riddle then? The answer, you see, lies in the answer to a very simple question.

And the question, you see, is: What should have been done with that old blind man? What kind of question is that, you say? He should have been venerated, of course, you say. He had warned the king of Yunnan about the danger to his throne and bed well before time. That a shepherd–swordsman would mess it all up was the king's fault, not the old blind man's. If possible, you say, he should have had a proper temple built for him, where he could keep on foretelling kings of the dangerous writs about their beds and thrones and, with some luck, he could have helped kings save their beds and thrones. I should be out there, you see. That is one way of looking at it. In fact, a commonplace way of looking at it, if I may say it so myself. Consider this: what if the king of Yunnan had dumped that old blind man in a dark pit as soon as he had been made aware of his wheezing existence? The king would never have been told or foretold about this father-killing-mother-fucking baby. The king would have never sent his newborn to be killed. The child would have grown up in the palace and once he grew up, he would have known his father by face, and that would certainly have helped in not murdering him – accidentally or otherwise. He definitely would not have climbed into his father's bed, for sure, and, even if by some mysterious turn of events the queen would have somehow ended up in his bed, he would have definitely recognized her as the mother who suckled and raised him. The future as foreseen by the old blind man would never have come to pass had the king never been told about it in the first place. And that, you see, brings us to another question. Did that old blind man do nothing more than read what the Moving Finger wrote, or was he just a pawn of the Finger on the chessboard of Time? That is to say, if I may take the poetry out of it, did the old blind man foresee the future, or was he its harbinger? If you ask me, I would definitely say it was the latter. That old wheezing blind man was no more than the Moving Finger's lackey striving to ensure the inevitability of what had been writ. There is no denying that. And I think some king or the other must have realized this too and passed on this knowledge as royalty passes so many other things onto their progeny across time and space – like madness, tyranny and this fascination with imprisoning their fathers and killing their brothers. Another rabbit hole there, you see. Nevertheless, back to here where we are. I think this is the reason I ended up here, in this pit full of darkness and wheezes. Prevention being better than cure, you see. What, you don't believe me? Pray, tell me then, why don't you see or hear of old blind men with memories of the future at royal courts anymore? You see, we used to be everywhere. And now, here we are. Exiles in the darkness and wheezes, you see. Believe or do not believe, it doesn't matter. You are stuck with me, remember, for the foreseeable future. No, no, you do not need any memory of the future to tell you that. It is just plain common sense. There is no escape from here, you see. What do I see for your future then? Well, I told you, it doesn't work that way. It is not as if I will hold your hand or sniff at your navel or lick your ears and all of your future would unravel before my blind eyes in a trance. No, sir, never. It is just memories, you see. They come as and when they like, like birds into traps. But this much I promise you, I will tell you whatever and whenever I remember – if I remember, that is, anything about you at all. For now, you see, it is just darkness and wheezes, wheezes and darkness.

17

The Pustule of Memory

The memory of light is now a pustule in my eyes. I close my eyes and there it is – a turgid, foetid mote of pain. I open my eyes and there it remains. As painful as before, if not more. It hurts. Oh, it hurts so bad!

It will burst, I keep telling myself, sooner or later it has to. All that pus of memory will drain and maybe then this darkness will not be as unbearable as it is now. Maybe then I will sit in my corner as blind as the wheezing old man is in his. Maybe blindness is what it takes to overcome this darkness …

But then, how do I know I am not blind already? How do I know that this pit is not awash with light right now and it is my blindness that keeps me from seeing it? Can a blind man even tell light apart from darkness?

'One can always tell,' the old man says as he clears his throat in anticipation of the barrage of words that are to follow. There is no stopping him now. 'One can always tell when it is dark. You see, it is the way darkness weighs on your eyes. Like regret weighs on the soul. Like the weight of wings in a cage. Nothing surprising there, you see, blindness does not let you see things. But darkness is something that you cannot see in the first place. You always perceive darkness only by how it weighs on your eyes. So, you see, blind, not blind – it doesn't matter. Although it must be said one will always prefer sight over blindness. It is quite pleasurable, you see, to think that one can see the light if given the opportunity. That there is always that possibility to see, even if you cannot presently, is far better than knowing one can never see the light. What? It is also painful, you say, given the circumstances we are in here? Yes, yes, of course it is. So painful for you. But then, you see, it is painful only because you know it is possible to replace it with the pleasure of sight. All you need is to get out somehow. Now, when you know such a replacement is not your option, what then are you left with? Darkness. Only darkness, you see. Days and nights full of it, like a snake's hole. Although, historically speaking, when all of us were sold to His Excellency – now wait a minute, what were we sold for? What was it that we cost? Seventy-five lakh rupees, six goats and three shawls? That was it, wasn't it? Or did I miss something? Ah yes! The horse, you see! Seventy-five lakh rupees, one horse, six goats and three shawls. That is it, right? Now, when we were sold for seventy-five lakh rupees, one horse, six goats and three shawls, it was all of us, blind and otherwise. You see, it wasn't as if His Excellency was offered any discount on his prospective blind subjects. It was the same rate for all, blind and otherwise. So there you have it, from the mouth of history itself – blind, not blind, it doesn't matter. When it comes to it, we all cost the same, you see. Although bad business for His Excellency by all accounts, it must be said: if only he were to have someone like me by his side, I could have told him how purchasing blind men would not fetch him the same returns as it would otherwise. As, for instance, weavers like you, you people fetch a good return, don't you? Money and horses and goats spent on people like you is what I call money and horses and goats well spent. I don't even need to have memories of the future to tell you that. Just some plain common sense, you see. But, truth be told, money spent on purchasing you in particular seems to have gone waste. As wasted as it has been on me, sitting useless as we both are in this pit. You see, you could be at a loom, weaving and earning His

Excellency some returns, as the rest of your ilk is doing already. But here you are, in this darkness. Yes, yes. I see you in darkness. I can! I can! I remember! I remember it all!' he cries suddenly, his voice no longer that staid stream of words that flowed and meandered in wayward leisure through the meadow of unrestrained thoughts. It has now changed into a sea at storm.

'I see you in the darkness, cutting off your thumbs!'

A terrible violence lurks underneath the surface of his tormented voice as it lashes at every word that rises from its restless waters.

'You will cut your thumbs off in the darkness.'

18

The King of Thumbs

Once upon a time, there lived three brothers. One was Beautiful, the second was Brains and the third was Brutal. Enamoured by the beauty of the first one, the High King of the land made him his chamberlain. And once Beautiful had the High King's ear, he whispered about his two brothers – how great they were, how useful they could be. Thus, the king had his chamberlain's brothers brought to the court and gave them appropriate stations. Quite befittingly, Brains was made a minister, while Brutal was made a general in the imperial army. As years passed, the fortunes of the three brothers kept rising. Brains was now the prime minister, Brutal was commander-in-chief of the royal forces, and Beautiful held a position second only to the throne.

And then the High King died.

The intrigue of ascendancy in the dead king's wake marred his succession. This brought their enemy marching to the border, ready to pounce and gobble up the kingdom. The realm plunged into chaos. The three brothers found this chaos much to their liking, for in it they saw an opportunity to reach for more.

First, it was Brains. He was no longer content with being just a prime minister. So, he planned and plotted, plotted and planned till the plots and plans, like pots and pans left on the fire for too long, got too hot for him to handle. Thus, he was assassinated in his chambers on a hot and humid night.

Then, it was Beautiful. Time had not been kind to him. It had marked its passage with wrinkles and pocks on his once pretty face. Jealous of the young faces that had started to appear at court, he took up his sword, mustered as many men as he could and marched on, not exactly sure what he intended to win or whom he intended to defeat. Consequently, it didn't take long for him to get himself as well as the men by his side killed. The exquisite bejewelled daggers of Beautiful and his acolytes being no match for the horrible crude swords that ripped apart their delicate bellies.

All that remained now was Brutal. He too, like his brothers, had seen the opportunity that the chaos had brought. But he, unlike his brothers, had also seen the chaos for what it really was – a maze. One had to step through it very carefully and very patiently; only then did one stand a chance to reach the other side and claim the prize. Brutal refused to be rash like Brains or foolish like Beautiful. He bided his time. Only when he was sure that the time was ripe, did he make his move. He reached out to the enemy at the border. They shook hands and the enemy marched into the kingdom. As the battle began, Brutal withheld the forces under his command from the battlefield. Those left to fight for the kingdom were soon routed and the enemy prevailed. Once the battle was over, the victorious enemy granted the title of King to Brutal in recognition of the great help he had provided to the victors. All he needed now was a kingdom. And he got one. He purchased one from the victorious enemy for a prize of seventy-five lakh rupees, one horse, six goats and three shawls.

Brutal now had a title and a land full of people to rule over; all that was left to make a proper king out of him was filling up the royal coffers. And there was only one place in his new kingdom that could fill them up – and fill them up really quickly. The vale. Its riches and treasures would be more than sufficient to fill up his coffers now and forever. The only problem were those vermin men and women who occupied that beautiful place. Filthy bastards who worshipped a strange foreign god; they would even eat their mothers for meat – if they were not doing it already, that is. He could have done away with them, get the land purified and consecrated once and for all. But then, he had paid good coin for each one of them. All that waste did not appeal to the frugal mind of King Brutal. So he decided that this scum of existence could eke out their disgusting lives as long as they paid for it. And pay they did – by reaping the fruits of their soil and the riches of their looms for King Brutal. In turn, he would provide them with enough food to survive another season of reaping. The coffers started to fill.

But then, one day, the hungry weavers at the loom started to get angry. If hunger is all that a day's toil will earn them, they started to murmur, why not earn the same at someplace else without the toil at least? They could beg, for instance. But King Brutal would have none of it. The weaver will be allowed to leave his loom, he decreed, only in his coffin – and that too only once his son fills up the empty seat. The coffers started to fill up again.

But then, the hungry weavers were at it again. Let us run away from this accursed vale, they started to murmur. King Brutal would again have none of it. He filled the mountain passes with his guardsmen. No sooner would a weaver appear there than he would be dragged back to his loom and whipped till he made up for the lost labour. If someone still managed to slip through – either to his death or to the other side – whatever he left behind – mother, sister, daughter – would have to pay. The coffers continued to fill.

But then, one day, a weaver was brought to King Brutal for punishment. No one knew what to do with him. No one could make him weave anymore. The King raged and raved. And then he raged and raved some more. And more. But no matter how much King Brutal raged and raved, there was no way of making the weaver weave again. Take him away,

King Brutal cried to his guardsmen finally. Take away this abomination. I am not King of this thumbless man. I am the King of Thumbs only.

19

The Cleaver

Heemal hangs by a rope. I try to pull her up but I cannot. I just cannot hold on to the rope. It keeps slipping through my hands. No matter how hard I try, the rope keeps slipping through my fingers. It is as if ... as if ... as if I have no thumbs! I look down at my hands. There are no thumbs! But these hands; they are not my hands! They are Abli Bab's! Yes, yes, Abli Bab's. 'Let us have your thumbs now,' Abli Bab says. 'It is easy. Just stretch your hands like this. Fingers separate, thumbs apart ...' I jerk my hands free from his grasp and run away. No, not my thumbs. No. No ... I keep running. It is so dark I cannot see where I am running to. I hit something. I stumble. I fall. I am at Abli Bab's feet. He helps me get back up, his hands on my shoulders. He smiles. 'It is so easy. Just a moment of pain, that is all. Here, take this and be done with it,' he says as he hands me a cleaver. The cleaver falls from my hand. I try to pick it back up but I cannot. It is so heavy. The more I try to pick it up the heavier it gets. The effort is too much for me, my hands start to tremble. My heart starts to pound. 'Please, not my thumbs.' I start to cry. 'Hush! Hush, now,' Heemal says as she takes my hand, 'You have nothing to worry about. Here, put your head on my lap. Everything will be all right.' Her voice is turning hoarse as she starts to wheeze. She opens a bronze box and takes out a cleaver from it. A blue cleaver. 'This will help,' she says with a heavy voice as her wheezing makes it difficult for her to speak. She holds me tight in her arms as Abli Bab grabs my right hand. He pins my hand, fingers separate, thumb extended, to the butcher's block. Heemal smiles as she runs her fingers through my hair. I want to cry aloud for help, but I do not. All I do is watch the cleaver rise high above Abli Bab's head with a fascination which is as horrible as it is livid. I keep watching in thrall as the cleaver makes its way down, all the way down to my thumb … I wake up with a painful cry.

'Dreaming about the thumbs again, eh?' the blind old man says between his wheezes.

'I cannot do it,' I cry as I open my eyes to the darkness, 'I will never be able to do it. I don't have it in me to cut my thumbs. I don't. I am not brave like them.'

'Brave? The ones who cut their thumbs are brave, you say? Ha ha ha ... What strange notions of bravery you have, my dear! You see, it is like saying I will cut off my head and you won't be able to slap me anymore. Ha ha ha ... Some bravery that, huh? Ha ha ha ... What hard-arse bravery! Ha ha ha ... You think bravery is what it takes to cut off one's thumbs? Bravery, eh? Ha ha ha ... Dear Lord, have some mercy on the brains of this one here! You think the King of Thumbs lets off the men who cut off their thumbs because they are brave? Is that what you think, you pea-brained little fool? Why, then the King of Thumbs must let go of all his brave enemies when he meets them in the battlefield. Well then, does he? Has he ever? Some king he would be if he lets something like bravery thwart him! Why, he would not even be a king in the first place if bravery is what it took to stop him. You see, it isn't bravery that makes one cut off his thumbs, no sir, believe me, it isn't. It sure as hell isn't. It is rather despair. Yes, yes, nothing but deep, dark despair that makes one cut his thumbs, not bravery. Despair, that perennial instigator of flagellation that often masquerades as bravery. You see, the King of Thumbs understands that. As he understands that one must not dare push anyone beyond despair. That is where monsters are born. In the bog marshes of terror beyond despair.

And history, you see, is full of kings gobbled up by such monsters. But you, my dear, you don't need to worry for now. You see, you have not known despair yet. You are just hurling down the darkness for now. But you will know despair. By God, you will. You see, there is nothing but despair at the bottom of darkness. And trust me, no dream can take you to such depths of despair as darkness eventually will.'

20

The Depths

'Dreams of the dark depths of despair. The despair of the dark depths of dreams. The depths of dark despair of dreams. The dark depths of despair of dreams. The depths of dark dreams …'

That wheezing old bastard, he is at it again. If only that infernal tongue of his were to be forced down his throat, this place would have some silence. But why should anything good turn up in here? Why should I have even a moment's peace?

I, as I have done many times before, get up and follow the wheezing. The blind old weasel, he senses me coming. He tries to stop the wheezing by holding his breath but ends up bursting into a fit of coughing so bad that he almost spits out his lungs. Scared, he tries to run away from me but I am too fast for him. Besides, in here, where could he run? It is almost too easy to catch him. I have him by the throat. I slap him as hard as I can. I hit his nose perhaps or maybe it is his ear. I slap him again and again. 'One of these days, I swear I will rip out your throat and chew those wheezing lungs of yours.'

'Yes. Yes, you will, you will. But not now, surely. Not this time, please,' he squeaks. I let go of his throat. He slips away. For a moment, there is complete silence. No words. No wheezes. 'But then, how will you rip out my throat without those thumbs, eh?' He taunts me with a chuckle as soon as he thinks he is out of my reach. Maybe he is correct. Maybe my thumbs are the problem, after all. Maybe to cut them off is to end this all … No, no, no. That son of a bitch, he has got into my head again. 'Shut up, you motherfucker,' I shout as I remain undecided on whether to catch him again or not. His response to my indecision is a wheezing chuckle that curdles the darkness all around.

It isn't worth it, I decide. In here, nothing is worth anything.

'Please get me out of here,' I pray to whoever is listening up there.

'Yes, yes. Please get him out of here,' the blind bastard cries in a mocking voice, 'Poor him, he needs to get out. He needs to save his precious little thumbs. You see, he no longer trusts himself with his thumbs.'

Suddenly, I feel so tired. So tired and so scared. I collapse onto the floor and start weeping. I don't know how long I can keep up with this.

'The depths of dark despair. The dark depths of despair. The despair of dark depths. The dark despair of ...'

The old blind bastard is at it again.

21

The Miracle

'You there?' a voice flits in on broken wings, earnest in its despair as it begs for some trust. But it doesn't fool me, I don't believe that voice. In here, I have been made a fool one too many times.

'This is me.'

Yes, it is you. Won't I recognize your voice? But I am not falling for it. I am not falling for one more sadistic charade conjured up by this dark, foetid swamp of delusions.

'It is me. It is me, Heemal.'

Of course, it is you. Who else could it be but you?

'I am here … well here … I am here to … I have come to get you out. Yes, I have. Believe me, I have. You just need to tell them a name … they will … they will let you out. Believe me, they will. But … you know … a name … you need to tell them a name, just a name … Believe me … You have to, you know.

Strange things have happened outside ... A miracle, they say ... No, no, not a miracle, we don't want them to get angry, but that is what everyone out there says it is – a miracle. It just happened, everyone knows and everyone calls it that – a miracle. And if you can ... well ... you know, just after you ... just after you slept ... I mean, just after you were taken away, this miracle, it happened at Haer Parbat ... it did ... that is what they say ... everyone says ... not on Haer Parbat itself, just below it. It had snowed so much, you remember ... Cold, frightful snow ... But then it was blue snow. Yes, at the foot of Haer Parbat, the snow turned blue. Anyone who touched it, his hand turned blue and anything that hand touched also turned blue ... a weird, obstinate blue that refused to go away no matter how much you tried to get rid of it ... An obstinate weird but beautiful blue, the sort of blue that is worthy of being called blue ... true blue, you understand ... The most beautiful blue that could ever be conjured up ... the kind of blue you can spend a lifetime searching for, like ... like, you know ... I knew ... I mean, as soon as I heard, I knew ... I thought I knew ... I mean ... it was like ... Then when the snow melted, a carpet beneath it all ... A carpet so blue you would not believe ... Nobody could. How? What? They said it was a piece of sky ... Fallen ... a miracle ... a sign ... a sign from

Makhdoom Saab himself ... At the foot of his exalted shrine ... a piece of sky for the destitute ... for the wretched ... relief for the tormented ... The word spread. People gathered. All sorts of people ... to gather under the sky ... the blessed sky ... just once, if not more ... crowds swelled ... Noisy crowds, angry crowds ... That is when they came for it from the fort. The miracle – the piece of sky – was confiscated. Who is going to pay for this carpet? That is what it was before the law, after all – a carpet, not a miracle. Not a piece of sky. Just a carpet. And the tax had to be paid for it. As it has to be paid for any other carpet. That is the law. But then, who would pay? Whose is the miracle? Who owns the sky? There were no answers. The law took its own course. No one responsible is everyone responsible. Everyone must pay the extra tax. That was the only solution. But then, even stranger things happened. Weavers left their looms ... Can you believe that? Karkhans empty. The weavers – every one of them – helpless ... All of them on the streets, raising voices, singing dirges under the blue sky ... the blessed blue sky ... It was a procession. It was a funeral ... And then they came again ... they came swooping down from the fort, angry and armed this time ... Such ugly news from everywhere ... Mayhem and misery. Death and wailing ... But ... but that wasn't the end of it. The men from the fort need answers. Who did this, they are asking everyone. Who is behind this mischief? Who is responsible for this treachery? But there are no answers ... only punishments ... All blue hands confiscated but still the fort is not satisfied. They need to do something more. They need to find someone. They keep on searching. Somebody has to pay for the treachery after all, so that everybody learns his lesson. There is someone behind all this ... there has to be ... If they could only get a name. Any name. And if it is worth it, there will be a reward ... whatever you ask for ... Even freedom from the dungeon ... Yes, yes, you can get out ... only a name ... just a name ... here, they are even allowing you to see my face as a proof of their earnestness ... Here, here, come here. You can see me by this hole. Here, follow my voice ...'

A hole in the dark sky! At last, a hole in this dark sky! The beam of light bursting through it so bright, it hurts to look at it, yet my eyes cannot get enough of it. I run to drink from it, to bathe in it, pour it all over my body – this celestial honey that oozes from that hole, this luminescent dew of heavens! But the old wheezing whoreson beats me to it. He is already under it, gathering its warmth in his cupped hands while the cobweb across his blind opaque eyes lights up.

'Get away, you son of a bitch, this is for me,' I shout as I push him away.

But he wriggles his way back in. 'This is mine, only mine. All mine,' he hisses.

'What is happening?' Heemal cries from up there somewhere. 'Can you hear me? We don't have much time. We need a name, please.'

'Go away, you infernal cur. Go back to your lair of darkness. Rot there and leave this to me,' I scream. But before I could push him away, this time he wraps himself tightly around me with his gnarled limbs. 'You cannot get rid of me,' he keeps sneering as he coils around me like poison ivy.

'A name, please. They are waiting.'

I catch him by his neck as I try to pick him off me. But he is too strong for me. I press down on his neck, my fingers finding the space around his throat as we struggle. His face is nauseously close to mine and it stirs up a lava of hate inside me.

'We don't have time. They will take me away anytime now. Please, just tell them a name. Any name. Please, for God's sake.'

My hands close around his throat. His eyes start to pop out and his face contorts itself into a different face. I have seen that face before. Yes, I have. I definitely have.

'A name. A name.'

Yes, yes, the name, the name. I am almost there. My hands around his neck turn tighter and tighter. That face! That face! The name almost on my lips. Just a little more effort. A little more …

'A name. Now. Say it now. Please, say it now. It is now or never.'

'Abli Bab! Yes! Yes! Abli Bab! ABLI BAB! ABLI BAB … ABLI BAB!'

22

The Gift

Restless, the waters of the Jhelum meander through the old city as if trying to find a way to avoid flowing to the other side. As if to free itself from the vicissitudes of its own ebb and flow, it was desperately trying to find a way to eat its own tail. But all that the Jhelum manages to do is twist and turn itself into knots as it flows through the old city. Its course a gash drawn by a wavering dagger held by an unsteady hand. A wound that threatens to tear the old city apart into two.

Seven bridges try to stitch this wound that is the Jhelum across the old city. Seven bridges separated by distance and time and history. Seven bridges, seven *kadals*. Each kadal bears the name of its builder. Amira Kadal, Habba Kadal, Fateh Kadal, Zaina Kadal, Aali Kadal, Nawa Kadal, Safa Kadal. Of the seven bridges, the middle one – the Zaina Kadal – has its own story to tell.

It is said that once, Zaina Shah – the Budshah, the great king – fell ill, so ill that he feared for his life. The fear only grew worse when this stubborn illness refused to respond to any of the treatments that his royal physicians and healers of the time could devise. Time was running out and everyone was running out of solutions. Just when the last candle of hope began to flicker, a frail man appeared in court and offered his services. Shri Bhat was his name and he was a pandit – a brahmin – by creed. His services were accepted despite the apprehensions about the services of an infidel. Death was at the door and if it took an infidel to keep the door closed, then so be it. Thus, the pandit commenced his treatment of the sultan and, to the relief of everyone (and the chagrin of some), the sultan responded well. God and his mysterious ways! Thence the road to recovery was swift and smooth. Soon enough, a healthy and grateful sultan asked Shri Bhat to name a gift for the immense service he had rendered to him and he would have it, come what may – that was a sultan's promise. Shri Bhat replied that since he had saved the sultan's life, only a gift as precious as life would be befitting. The reply left the sultan perplexed. Where could I find such a gift, he wondered. A gift as precious as life, did such a gift even exist? Should the sultan renege on his promise and ask Shri Bhat to name a different gift? But then, he wasn't Budshah for no reason. He was going to keep his promise come what may. He thought and thought. And soon enough, he realized only a gift as indiscriminate as life could be as precious as life. And what better gift is as indiscriminate as life than a bridge? Just like life, a bridge lets everyone pass – the faithful, the infidels; the rich, the poor; the firm, the infirm – without any fear or favour. The sultan had found the answer. He finally had a gift as precious as life and he would bestow this gift not just upon Shri Bhat but all of his people – the believers as well as the infidels. The gift as indiscriminate as life. The gift as precious as life. The gift of Zaina Shah. The bridge of Zaina Shah. The Zaina Kadal.

But it wasn't easy building this bridge, for the waters of the Jhelum ran deep and treacherous. Any attempt to dam those waters to raise the piers for the bridge would submerge the old city on either bank. Nevertheless, a sultan's promise is a sultan's promise. A way was found eventually. The sultan ordered old boats filled with stones to be sunk in the Jhelum at the site where the bridge was to be built. As boat after stone-filled boat sunk at the designated spot, they started to pile up. Soon, the sunken boat piles were high enough to break out through the surface of the water. These piles were the foundations over which logs of sturdy deodar trees cut, hewn and brought down the Jhelum, were laid one upon another to form the piers. And over these piers the spans of the bridge were laid. The gift of Zaina Shah Budshah was complete.

From one of the protruding logs of this bridge – of this gift as precious as life – hangs Abli Bab.

23

The Bargain

'Come, that is enough,' Heemal whispers in my ear as I stare at the rotten body hanging from the Zaina Kadal. It has been left hanging as a lesson for all those who pass by. It will be left hanging as a warning to all those who pass by.

'It is enough. Let us leave now.'

But I don't want to leave. I want to keep looking at those piled up logs of the bridge that keep protruding like accusing fingers with their tips neatly snipped off. I want to keep looking at the uneasy noose that sways with every gust of air that blows, mocking the lifelessness that hangs from it.

I don't want to face the moment that comes after this.

'Come now,' Heemal insists as she leads me away, 'it is about time. We have a long way to walk.'

Wherever is left to walk to? Wherever to must we walk? Heemal doesn't answer. She just keeps walking ahead, but turns back to look at me every now and then to make sure I am following her. To make sure the gossiping waters of the Jhelum that rush by our side do not carry me back. From Zaina Kadal to Fateh Kadal, from Fateh Kadal to Habba Kadal, we walk without uttering a single word, without breaking our step. If only we could keep walking like this till we reach the end of time! But Amira Kadal is as far as we go. Heemal stops. 'This is it,' she says, 'this is where we part.'

I don't understand. It makes no sense. What is there to part from?

'You see that building over there,' Heemal mutters as her left hand clenches into a fist while the right hand points at the back of a dirty brown building standing ominously a few paces away from us. It is an ugly large house whose bricks and wood seem unable to keep it together. The house seems to overflow its walls and windows as if a beast had swallowed a prey only to find his belly too small to contain it.

'It is a brothel and I have sold myself to it. Giving them a name was only one half of the bargain to set you free, the other half was to pay up. And I had nothing else left to sell except myself.'

The depths of dark despair. The dark depths of despair. The despair of dark depths. The darkness of despairing depths …

'It is all right. It didn't turn out to be a bad bargain after all. Only now, I cannot decide which was the better trade – selling you only to fail to get Father back or selling myself to get you out only to lose you forever.'

'Come with me.'

'And where shall we go? Where will they let us go? You have your own brothel waiting for you. Your karkhan. Don't mistake you getting out of that dungeon for your freedom. They will drag you back to your karkhan sooner or later. Eventually, we all end up in brothels. It is just a matter of time.'

'Come with me.'

'Go now. Go away. Run. Hide. And keep running and hiding as much as you can. As long as you can. That brief running, hiding chance is all I have been able to purchase for you.'

'Come with me.'

'Are you even listening to me? I cannot go with you. Why don't you understand! I cannot run. Even if I could, I don't want to run. I am tired. I am tired of being a daughter when my father needs a son, now more than ever. I will only slow you down. Besides, do you think the fort will allow losses at the brothel and the karkhan at the same time? Alone, you have a chance to run and hide, at least for some time. Together we don't.'

'Come with me.'

'Why don't you listen to me? Stop this madness. Go away. Run. Hide. Go now. Go away.'

'Come with me.'

'For God's sake, don't make me regret selling myself. As if the regret of selling you isn't misery enough already.'

24

The Sting

Running and hiding. Hiding and running, where else could I have ended up but here in this cave? This miserable cave where days are full of ennui like that of fattened vultures lingering around inexhaustible corpses. And the nights, the nights are full of the black sands of darkness eager to blow into my eyes. I try not to let the sand in. I try to find the oasis of sleep to while away this sandstorm of darkness. But every time I close my eyes, a log of wood pokes at my eyeballs. A roughly hewn log of deodar that protrudes like an accusing finger with its tip snipped off. There is nothing to do but to keep the eyes wide open. Helpless thus, the sands of darkness rush in and pour themselves into a desert of despair in my wide-open eyes. The solace, if any, in this dark wilderness are the wheezes. Yes, those infernal wheezes that used to drive me mad. But now, they are my only comfort. My only twinkling stars in this everlasting darkness. I long for them to fill up the cave every night with the hope that those wheezes will lead me to words, as they always did in the past. Words of any kind – as long as they are words. As long as they fill the terrible silence of this dark cave. But there are only wheezes, no words. Not even one. 'Talk to me,' I beg, 'Talk to me, please.'

'What is left to talk about now?' he sulks as he recedes into the depths of silence, leaving behind only the wheezes. But I keep begging. I keep insisting. 'Say something. Anything.'

But he says nothing. He doesn't relent. Stubborn as only he can be, no begging is going to change his mind. Nobody knows that better than I do. I am about to give up when it comes to me – the invitation that his restless tongue cannot resist. 'If you do not want to talk to me, don't, but what about a story at least? Tell me a story, please.'

'A story?' his words break through his wheezes. Yes, yes, I knew he could not resist such an invitation.

'Well, no harm in telling a story, I guess.' There he goes.

'Stories and water to drink, I say, should never be kept to oneself. You see, they are meant to be shared. No use hoarding them. They ooze out anyway. So a story, you say. Well then, I have a story for you. The story of Shraz the Beast. Yes, yes, the story of a beast. You see, in darkness, nothing makes as much sense as stories of beasts. The shraz, it is said, has the head of a man over the body of a lion. Now, now, there is no need to be disgusted, there absolutely isn't. You see, this Shraz might have the abominable body of a beast, but he has a tender, foolish heart in his breast. A tender, foolish, throbbing heart. You see, the beasts, they must always have tender, foolish, throbbing hearts in a story – otherwise, it may as well be history. And you don't want me to talk about history now, do you? Of course you don't. I understand that, you see. You have nothing personal against history. Nobody has. It is just that who would want to chase something that is already tied to us as a dog to its tail? You see, that is what history is in a cave full of darkness. A dog chasing its tail. That and nothing more. No sir, we sure as hell don't want dogs chasing their tails in here. What we rather want is a story. A proper story. The story of Shraz the Beast with a tender, foolish, throbbing heart. He opens his eyes and the first thing he sees is the Moon, that silver seductress of the sable skies that has led many a poet astray, making them jump off their cliffs of metaphors and similes. Yet, none seem to be the wiser for it, you see. No one seems to learn a lesson. Least of all our Shraz. For no sooner does he see the bright Moon draped in her silver gossamer than he falls in love with her. You see, it may not have been the love of similes and metaphors, but it was love all right. The primeval, aboriginal kind. The type of love whose longing is so painful that it drives you mad. There is no helping that, you see. There is no helping Shraz's longing for the Moon despite all the pain that comes with it. You see, falling in love is just like being stung by a bee. The bee might have stung you, yet you cannot help but reach out for her. Run after her. You see, only she has got the honey to spread over that wound. She is your only chance at whatever relief you may get. Misery comes from the bee, as does the salve. Thus, Shraz runs after the Moon who remains perched high above, disdainfully and perpetually out of reach. But that is not how she appears to the Shraz at all, you see. No sir, she doesn't. For Shraz, she is up there waiting for him, with all the honey and salve that he needs. All that he must do is climb up that mountain peak to get close to her and then he can have her. That is what he must do. And that is precisely what he does, you see. He climbs that mountain peak in all his beastly frenzy. Once he is at the top of the peak, he beholds the Moon in all her uninhibited, naked glory. Her silver tresses almost touching Shraz's panting lips. The lunacy of desire takes over completely. It leads Shraz to the edge of the summit, tantalizingly close to the Moon. He can almost touch her. A little more and he can have her … Just a little more … There, there, almost there … A leap of faith … He jumps, but the Moon slips, keeps slipping away, as Shraz lands with broken bones and torn flesh on the ground. You see, that is how it is always. Lovers ending up broken and dead on the ground. There is no helping that. Anyway, the irresistible feast of flesh seasoned with desire and gurgling pools of red blood laid out at the bottom of the peak brings the hungry worms out of their holes. They gorge on Shraz. All of him. Every bit of him. And the fever of desire passes on to these hungry worms. The body of Shraz is not enough for them, so they start eating each other up. As each worm gobbles the other up, they grow fewer in number but bigger in size. They keep gobbling up each other until only a single one is left. A single monstrously engorged worm. The last one, you see, who can neither gobble anyone nor be gobbled up by anyone. Yet, we are not done with him. You see, all that blood and flesh and bones inside him begin to shape up into a beast by the memory of desire that they share. This beast stretches itself and tears apart that last worm from within. Once out, the beast opens his eyes. The first thing he sees is the Moon and no sooner he sees the bright Moon draped in her silver gossamer than he falls in love with her all over again. You see, there is no helping that. And as before, he starts to climb the highest peak to reach out to her. Shraz, every time he opens his eyes, will do what he always does. That is what makes him Shraz. There is no helping that.'

25

The Exorcism

There is no helping that. They are trapped in my head, the murmurs, the noise. That is all that this cave could offer me. Nights full of wheezes and days full of murmurs. Wheezes I could do with but the noise of these murmurs, it makes me want to break open my skull. It is as if someone had burst open a wasp's nest in my head. The wasps scutter to get away, only they cannot find a way out. Trapped, they keep buzzing and hovering all around all day long in anger. Only if they could burst out of my head somehow and be gone forever!

'There is no helping that,' he says, his voice rising above the mist of wheezing. 'You could split open your skull to let the wasps fly away but it is not wasps that are in your head. You see, those murmurs you keep hearing all day long – they are nothing but flesh-worms whispering to each other. Yes, yes, flesh-worms, indeed. This cave is full of them. Flesh-worms are what you find under a rock. And that is what you will find under us, beneath this rock of a hillock. Flesh-worms spawning in the skull of the one who lies there, crushed under the weight of centuries. They creep and crawl out of his rotting mouth all the way up here and through those ears of yours, they have found a way into your skull. There they are now, inside a fresh skull. And there they will remain whispering to each other, spawning generation after generation, all of them murmuring all along.'

'Wasps buzzing or worms whispering, whatever the hell they are and whatever the hell they are doing, all I care about is how to get rid of them,' I say.

'You need to exorcise them.'

'Exorcise?'

'Yes, exorcise, indeed.'

'And how does one do that?'

'Well, you see, what is the first thing that any exorcist does at an exorcism? What is the first thing he asks the tasrufdar, or the unwelcome jinn?'

'What?'

'The first thing that the tasrufdar is asked is what they want. That is the key to the exorcism. In fact, that is the key to everything, be it jinns or tasrufdar or people. What does someone want? You find an answer to that and you know everything there is to know about anyone. And once you know everything about anyone, you control the strings of that puppet.

So there you go. Listen to the worms in your skull. Listen to their whispers and see what they want.'

It may not be much, but it is worth a try.

I close my eyes and try to eavesdrop. But there is too much of it – the buzzing, the murmuring. It is like dozens of criss-crossing streams at the same time. You try to dip into one only to find yourself carried away by the other. It is tricky, but if you manage to swim along one, you soon know how to swim through and across all of them. It takes its time, but I hold on to one of them for long enough to swim through it. Slowly but steadily the buzzing and the murmuring resolve into words. I press my ears closer. The murmuring is now a sing-song. A chant. A taalim?!

Two knots of red regret, six knots of grey grief. And one knot of dark dreary disbelief.

'There you go,' he says as he chuckles and wheezes at the same time.

'No! No! Not that accursed taalim again! I am done with it. I am forever done with it,' I cry as I try to bury that sing-song under the murmurs. As I try to get out of those raging streams.

'There is no helping that now. The jinn is out of the bottle, you see. There is no unhearing that taalim once you hear it. He he he ...'

Indeed, there isn't. The more I try, the worse it gets. All the murmurs, all that buzzing is just taalim now. The chants all around only getting stronger.

Seven knots of white woe, five knots of silver sorrow. Two knots of freckled fear. Then four knots of dark despair …

The wheezing bastard tricked me into this and there is no going back now. There is no undoing the taalim now.

'I cannot do it. I will never weave anything again.'

'It doesn't matter what you can or cannot do. What matters is what you cannot help but do. Now, listen to those worms. Listen to their taalim of woe and give them what they want.'

'What the hell do they want?'

'What does a taalim always want? A knot. That is what every chant of taalim ever cries for. A knot after a knot after a knot. And that is what you will give them – and pray they leave you alone. You see, that is how the exorcism is done.'

I rage and I rave. I rave and I rage. But there is no escaping the taalim. There is no escaping the loom. I grab a handful of warp threads and tie them in a knot. Then I tie another. And another …

There is no helping that.

26

The Trap

Knot after knot, this tree grows. The Tree of Life – that is what it should have been. That is what grows on every carpet where the seed of that blessed, bountiful tree of Paradise is planted in the soil of the warp and weft and nurtured by drop after drop of knots. A seed dreamt long ago by someone as he failed to behold the eternity of the garden of Paradise. A seed passed on in the song of taalim to be knotted and nourished on innumerable looms ever since. A seed that sprouts each and every time into a beautiful tree with branches laden with fruits of all seasons, and boughs that bear nests for birds of all feathers. A tree full of life. The Tree of Life. But that is not what has grown on my loom. How could it? For the tree on my loom doesn't grow from the seed of a dream; rather, it erupts from a nightmare, from the mouth of a flesh-worm. It grows on the top of a hillock, its roots, like the talons of a vulture, digging deep through the flesh of the rock to suck on the lake of blood and bile beneath it. The sap of bitter tears oozes from its parched bark. And no one dares to nest on its unwelcome boughs as severed thumbs grow all over them like sharp thorns. Its branches protrude like accusing fingers, with their tips neatly cut off, and the only fruit that hangs from those branches are nooses. It is not the Tree of Life that has germinated on my loom but it is rather a tree of death. An ugly, horrible tree that should make you look away in disgust – only, it doesn't. There is an earnest appeal in its ugliness. A fascination in its horridness, as if one were staring into the mirror of death and decay. It is a terrible beauty that this carpet bears. A beauty so cold and so dreadful that it settles on my eyes like hoar-frost. What if this is what it takes to fly?

'No, this will not fly. It is trying to lure you,' he whispers in my ear before his wheezing takes over.

'What is?'

'That carpet. It is luring you. But no surprises there. You see, that is what every carpet is in the first place. An allurement. An entrapment. That is what every carpet that has ever been woven is. And that is what every carpet that shall ever be woven will be. A trap.'

'What do you mean? I don't understand. How can a carpet be a trap? It makes no sense.'

'But it does. It makes perfect sense. It would make sense to you too if only you could tell me why the first carpet was woven at all.'

'I cannot.'

'Well then, we must go to where it all began. You see, you can make sense of something only if you know its beginning. You may see the pearl and you may see the oyster, but unless you know its beginning you will never understand why the pearl makes no sense without a grain of sand. So that is where we must start – from the first grain of sand – from the beginning. And it all began much before our Amir-e-Kabir, blessed be his name, bought those weavers to our vale; much before the beloved Zaina Shah Budshah bestowed the gift of weaving on us all; much before this gift turned out to be a curse for all of us. It began much, much before all that in a place far away, where a king reigned happily on his throne. For just above his throne, a huge diamond shone. A diamond so bright that it hurt the sight. A diamond so beautiful as if it had stolen heaven's light. The diamond shone, the King sat on his throne and all was right with the world. That is, until a thief decided to sneak into the palace under the cloak of the night and steal that diamond bright. But he could not run far, this thief. He could not keep the diamond from shining like a star. Thus, wherever he ran, he found the palace guards not far behind on his trail as the diamond shone like the Pole Star from afar. Running and panting, the thief had to decide quick whether it was to be the diamond or his own self that should take the fall. For the thief, having reached the end of the road, stared down from a cliff tall. His decision was swift. The diamond took the fall as it shattered on the rocky plain below into a hundred pieces small. The king was aghast. His precious pretty diamond was all but lost. All that remained were pieces so small that none of them could contain the whole light with which the diamond shone. Each part could only a part of that light hold. A red here, a blue there, a violet here, an ochre there, a lilac here, a peach there – all of it spread below the king as if it were a garden of flowers in full bloom. The king stared at it all. And he kept staring all day long. And the next day. And the next. So on and so on. The king on the cliff kept staring at what remained of his diamond bright while the throne far away from his sight remained empty and the palace desolate. The courtiers grew desperate. That is, until a man came to the fore. "Give me time," he said, "and I will bring back the king to his throne." The man brought cotton and silk and wool and tied them into knots with a little red here, a little blue there, a little violet here, a little ochre there, a little lilac here, a little peach there. Thus, a carpet was born. The first carpet ever woven. And this carpet was sprung before the King like a trap. He stared at it as if he were staring down the cliff. And thus was he lured back to his palace. He sat on his throne as the carpet was kept spread before him day and night. All was right with the world once again.'

So that is what it is! Is that what it has been all along? A trap and nothing more? That is what that loom is. Nothing but a spider's web! To lure? To trap? No more, I say. No more. It ends now. This carpet, this loom, it all ends now. I bring down the loom to pieces and tear the carpet away. I drag the carpet from the cave. I drag it all the way up to the ledge of Haer Parbat, where I throw it down with as much vehemence as a prisoner throws away their shackles. And with as much relief as well. Free, free at last, I start to run. I run down Haer Parbat. I run up the Jhelum. I run past all its seven bridges one by one. I run till I stand before a house. An ugly, dirty house whose walls and windows seem unable to contain it.

As dawn breaks, I knock on the door.

27

The Door

I knock on the door. I keep knocking on the door.

'Whose mother has died at the door?' someone cries from inside. 'Hold it till noon,' another one shouts with a laugh. 'A few winks of sleep for God's sake, that is all I ever ask for.' 'Stop that noise, you cunt's mole.' 'At this hour, the door is all you get to bang.' 'Leave us alone.' 'Too early for even a cock to rise.' 'Somebody call the fort.' 'Nettles in your father's grave.' 'Snakes in your arsehole.'

The voices rise and fall. All sorts of voices, all sorts of curses try to get me away from the door. But I keep knocking. I keep knocking till it opens. A man with a cleft lip stands at the door.

'Now, now, who do we have here?'

The tired corners of his lips tell me how forced the smile on his face is, how practised his enthusiasm

– all tricks of his trade. 'Well, dear friend, you know it is too early for the business, don't you? But for you, I will make an exception. Only for you and only this once.'

'Where is Heemal?'

'Of course. Of course. Whatever you wish for, my good friend. All in good time. But first, why don't you let me offer you something much better. Something that you yourself don't know how much you need. A fresh flower from the north. You won't rue even a single penny spent on her. Just come and take a look. It costs nothing to look, eh?'

'I have only come for Heemal. Please just bring her to me.'

'Patience, my friend, patience. Why eat brinjals when you can have peaches! Trust me, my friend, trust me on this and I swear you will never again ask for Heemal or, for that matter, anyone else.'

'For God's sake, why don't you understand? I need to see Heemal. No one but her.'

'Now, now, there is no need to get angry, my dear. Move on if you don't like the wares, friend.'

'Get me Heemal, you son of a bitch, or I will chew your liver right here, right now.'

'Hold your horses, you horny bastard. Let me make this very clear for you. There will be no Heemal today. Not for you, anyway. Take what I am offering or off you go with that squirming pizzle of yours. Got that?'

I punch him in the face.

'You crazy motherfucking cunt sore!' he swears as his kick sends me rolling away from the door. 'This is what I get for being so nice to you! Go away, you sodden son of Gomorrah. Be gone from here. If I ever see your face again at this door, I will hang you by your cock and choke you with your own balls. Get lost, you fucking faggot.'

The door closes shut. And I sit there. Beside the door. My head sinks into my knees. I know not what else to do. I know not where else to go. I remain where I am as the embers of dawn kindle into the morning.

As the morning turns into raging noon, I still remain where I was. People come and people go. The door opens and closes with irregular frequency. Crackles and cackles rise and fall behind the door as if someone had sprinkled a handful of water over boiling oil. But I remain where I was. Every now and then the cleft-lipped man appears at the door to check whether I am gone. And every time he finds me here at his doorstep, he spits at me and curses me under his breath.

It is almost midnight when they arrive, the pack from the fort. The cleft-lipped man receives them at the door. 'Oh, look who has arrived, finally!' he cries with mock exuberance.

'You pompous pimp, you think we remain at your beck and call?' says one from the pack.

'No, I don't. But I hadn't sent for you to come to my father's funeral either now, did I?'

'Enough with the drama already, what did you call us for?' says another from the pack.

'This,' the man says, pointing at me, 'this is what I have been trying to call you for since the morning. All day long, this son of a bitch has been sitting there like a dog. All day, I tell you. Right from dawn. This fucking freak, he didn't even move to pee or shit. Take this whoreson away from my door right now.'

The pack doesn't even bother to look at me. Why should they? I might as well have been a pile of cow dung stinking at the door for all they cared.

'And what makes your highness assume it is the fort that should be cleaning shit from your threshold?'

'Shouldn't you? He is as much my shit as he is yours. His presence at my door is a bad sight for the customers. That means bad business. Fall in earnings. And when earnings fall, they don't just fall for me now, do they?'

'And what about when the earnings fall for the fort only; you don't seem to mind it then, do you?'

'What do you mean?'

'Twenty-three whore licenses registered for your brothel but how long have you have been paying the fort weekly profits for only twenty-one of those?'

'How many times do I need to tell you that two of them are not working anymore? The blight made them useless. Not a single penny to be made between those legs anyhow. Nobody wants to pay for stinking cunts ripe with blight. Or does someone? And if you don't want to take my word for it, then be my guests and go fuck those two yourselves and take whatever profit you make. Better still, take those two to the fort and earn whatever you can from them. Don't pay me a single penny. Just get them off my back and you will have nobody as grateful as me for that service.'

'The fort is not a brothel, this is.'

'Then help me run it like a brothel. A stinking pile of disgusting shit at the door doesn't help with that, does it? Just have him gone from here and let me make money for all of us.'

'No, we won't. The orders are clear. No help will be provided till you get your house in order first. If you cannot manage things, then leave. We can have someone else in your place. Someone who knows how to get things done without excuses.'

That is it. The pack is done with the cleft-lipped man. They ride away.

'Devil's burning balls!' the man shouts after them and slams the door shut behind him as he walks back in. The lights are put out and the creaking house starts to sink into a sadistic silence for what remains of the night.

28

The Benefit

Another dawn breaks. Another morning passes by. One more noon carries me to the twilight shores of the night as I keep sitting by the door. For the umpteenth time, the door opens. This time, the cleft-lipped man walks out with a bowl in his hands.

'Here, eat. You must be hungry,' he says as he hands me the bowl, 'Go on. Eat. Don't test my patience.'

I eat. He sits on the steps by the door. 'You have to leave from my door, you understand that, don't you? You are bad for business. Very bad. If only you knew how bad. It should have been at least forty customers for today by this time. Forty, you understand? But what is the count for the day? Seventeen,' he shakes his head as he emphasizes the number. 'Just seventeen! Imagine that. By God, that is terrible. If only I could give you what you want!'

'Heemal. That is all I want.'

'Yes, of course you do. But it just cannot be done. I would let you have her if it were up to me, I swear, but there is nothing to be done with her. Absolutely nothing. You can have anyone else you like. Just have a look. One better than the other. And I would only charge half. I can't give you a better deal than that.'

'All I want is Heemal.'

'For fuck's sake, why don't you understand! There is nothing to be done with her. Absolutely nothing! Here, I offer you one shot with anyone else you like. Come in and choose whomsoever you fancy. Hell, I won't even charge you. Just be done with it quickly and leave this door, for devil's sake.'

'I am not here for all that. I need to see Heemal. Just this once and I will be gone from here.'

'You want to just see her? Just see her? Did I hear that right?'

'Yes. Yes.'

'You mean you want to just see her? Did I get that right?'

'Just see her once and that will be all.'

'Just see her and that too only once you say, right?'

'Yes. Yes. Just once.'

'And then you will be gone?'

'Yes. Yes. I swear I will be gone. I swear by the graves of all the saints.'

'Well, why not then! It isn't as if I haven't tried everything else. If this is what it takes to get rid of you,' he sighs, 'come along then.'

He gets up and I follow him as he walks around the house, away from the door. We walk to what looks like a small shed a few paces away from the house. A stable by the looks of it, or an abandoned cowshed. The cleft-lipped man unlocks the door of this shed and stands there.

'This is as far as I go. I am not going to go in there, not for a king's treasure. And I would advise you do the same. Don't go in there. It isn't worth it. Just listen to me, get away from here. As far away as you can. It just isn't worth it.'

But I remain there. Unwavering, unmoving.

'All right then, if this is what you want to get yourself into, go ahead; the door is all open but don't you dare to blame me after this. In you go. You will find her inside. It won't be difficult. There are only two of them in there. Do what you have to do and be quick about it.'

I step inside. It is dark. Darker than the fading evening outside. It takes a moment for my eyes to get used to this darkness. A moment and I see the faint outlines of bodies lying supine on the ground in the two corners of the wall opposite me. I walk over to the one that is breathing hard. Harsh, laboured breathing but still breathing. The other one holds little hope. A mop of dishevelled hair hides this one's face. Ample hair in all shades of black, some of it almost grey. The hair seems to be the only thing abundant about her, the rest of her body has shrunken to its skeleton, as if someone had peeled away all the flesh underneath her skin. I push aside the hair; it is Heemal all right. I know it is her despite the melange of sores that has left her face unrecognizable. A cry escapes her lips as I push away the hair from her face and in the process my hand touches a sore or two despite my caution. She starts to open her eyes. It is a painful struggle but she manages somehow. 'You!' she gasps as she sees me. 'It is really you, isn't it?' she asks me in a daze as she raises her fingers and caresses my face to reassure herself that I am not just a deception conjured by her desperate, bleary eyes. Her fingers are hot. Her hand is burning. Her whole body is burning with fever.

'Take me away, please. Don't leave me here this time.'

A thick teardrop spills from the corner of her eye and slithers rapidly over the sores on her left cheek. Its salt makes her wince with pain.

'Are you done in there?' the cleft-lipped man cries from the door, 'It is time to leave.'

I don't know what to say to him. I keep looking at Heemal's face. I keep looking at whatever is left of it. She has closed her eyes again. She looks as if she is sleeping but for the desultory moans that keep rising from her mouth. Each moan weaker than the one before but more painful, as if she were giving up her soul one breath at a time ...

'Do you hear me? You got to get going. Don't make me regret this.'

'I can't leave without her,' I blurt out somehow.

The man slaps his forehead. 'There you go, that crazy talk again. I knew you were making a fool out of me. You swore, you bastard. You said just once and you will be gone, didn't you?'

'I will leave. I swear I will. But I can't leave her here. Not like this. Just let me take her with me.'

'Have you gone mad? Are you even listening to what you are saying? Take her away! Do you know how much she cost me? One hundred rupees for her permit papers. Yes, you heard that right – one hundred rupees! Have you even ever heard of that much money? Plus, twenty-five rupees in cash she took in hand. Then add to that all the boarding and lodging charges. And she didn't even earn me back half of that yet. Even if I, in fucking generosity's name, were to take all that loss, how am I going to explain it to the fort? How in the devil's damned distress am I going to explain to the fort why I let go of a whore from this brothel? Would they believe in my devil fucking generosity? Rather, would they even let me have some devil fucking generosity? That doesn't go with the job, does it? That is not how this business works. That is not how the fucking fort will let anyone run this house.'

'Listen, listen. Hear me out first. Just hear me once. If you keep her here, you are still running losses, aren't you? She isn't going to earn anything for you, you know that. You know that better than anyone else. She is of no use to you any more. And yet you have to pay the fort their weekly dues. You have to and you will as long as she remains here. You cannot do anything about that. But if you let her go with me you can tell the fort she ran away. You won't have to pay them till they find her. And when they find her, I doubt she will make it back here. What is the punishment for runaways anyway? Dungeons? Hanging? In either case, you cut your losses. You get rid of her. And you get rid of me too. Because there is no way I am leaving your door without her.'

'Is that a threat?'

'Call it whatever you like. I am taking Heemal from here. Now you can get some benefit out of it or you can do yourself some harm. It is for you to decide.'

'Well,' he says as he scratches his chin, 'I am always in for some benefit.'

29

The Boat

Through the water the boat furrows its path. All it leaves behind is a trail of brief disquietude. A momentary disturbance before the water returns hurriedly to its overwhelming insouciance, just like the universe does, after every death.

Rocking and swaying, the boat moves forward, its boatman perched on its prow, his paddle laid upon his knees, resting in his lap. The boatman need not put in any effort as the Jhelum carries his boat downstream all by itself. Only the moans wringing out of Heemal in my arms disturb his pensive repose every now and then. 'Tch tch tch,' he clucks under his breath every time he hears her moan. Is it pity? Is it regret? I do not know. I can't tell. It was definitely pity when he had called to us at the ghat. 'She ill?'

he had asked as he had found Heemal bundled in my arms on the steps of the ghat by the Amira Kadal at dawn. That was only as far as we had got from the brothel. I knew not where to go from there. I didn't know where to take Heemal.

'She is ill.' He had answered his question himself after a moment's pause. 'Take her to the shrine of Makhdoom Saab. The saint will provide. He always does. To everyone. My sister was almost given up for dead, but she found her succour at the blessed saint's tomb. This one will also find relief there, by the grace of God. You just take her to the shrine. I can row you till the Aael Kadal if you want. I am going there anyway. You can carry her from there to the shrine.'

Shrine, yes, I am tethered to that shrine. To there I must return every time. To there we must go one more time.

'Tch tch tch,' the boatman mutters as the boat glides. We have reached the Zaina Kadal. I dare not look up. As the boat passes under the bridge, the boatman sings a song:

Mael-e-maej rachnas kong-a-kustaure
Douda saeti aesim tan nawaan
Soui paan lougmo raah musafirae
Kaensi ma ravein shoure paan

What my parents brought up on saffron and musk
And bathed in nothing less than milk
That same body now withers on the road –
If only the bliss of childhood were never to be lost.

It is an old song. One among the many sung by that ill-fated last queen of ours for her exiled king. Zoon, who became Habba Khatoon, only to rue the loss of her love in song after plaintive song. All of which she sang in vain. Her king never came back. He was lost beyond the mountains while she pined away. Her songs were all that was left behind. Songs that have been rowing ever since, across the river of time. Songs that are just brief disturbances before the universe returns to its eternal indifferent silence.

The boatman sings all the way to the Aael Kadal. Once there, he docks his boat. I carry Heemal to the shore. Her body no more than a heap of feathers in my arms. She moans and the boatman clucks under his breath, 'tch tch tch'. He rows back and away with the paddle in his hands, swift and strong, all set for another song.

Haer Parbat looms large in the distance. I lift Heemal on to my back and start to walk. Men and women pass us. Men and women of all kinds. Some pass by with a sad smile, some shake their heads and keep turning back. Some pass without a glance. Only one moves along beside me. An old hag bent double over the walking stick in her hand. Her steps fall in step with mine as she too carries a burden on her back – the burden of her old age. We tread along.

'Where are you taking her?'

Up there, I point with my eyes to the top of Haer Parbat.

'To Makhdoom Saab's shrine? Yes, yes, you must. It will do her good. The soil of the blessed tomb is a cure for all ailments except age. But who knows, there might be something else up there for old age too. I search for it there every day. I am not one to give up. But let us hurry now. There is anger in the air. And we don't want to be caught up in all that trouble. We who cannot outrun the storm must keep our distance at least.'

What is she even talking about?

'Why, haven't you heard, my son? People are gathering at Haer Parbat. Angry, outraged people from everywhere. They are rushing there by the minute. One more carpet has been found. One more carpet that does not look like it was born of the labour of a human hand. This time, it is something horrible. An obscenity. An abomination. An outrage. Oh, the horror of it all!'

30

The Abomination

'An abomination! An obscenity! An outrage! Oh, the horror of it all! I say, the horror of it all. You have to only look at it once to see the horror. What disgrace! What distortion! I have never heard profanity like that. I have never seen a perversion like that. The Tree of Life – the tree of blessed Paradise – violated like that! That too, right under the blessed shadow of the sacred shrine! A sacrilege! A sacrilege! God have mercy on us all. Who does that? Who violates the sanctity of divine order? The devil, I say. The devil, that greatest transgressor of us all. Who else would dare to damn his soul with a desecration like that? But then, how could someone as perfidious as the devil weave something so sincere? How could Eden's outcast weave something so sublime? He could not. How could he? If he could, the snares and traps he lays for us in this mortal world would not be snares and traps at all, they would be miracles. Yes, miracles! For that is what that carpet is. Abominable, yes. Ugly, yes. But it isn't a snare. It isn't a trap. It is a miracle. There is no denying that, no matter what everyone else says. A horrible miracle but a miracle nevertheless. It reaches out to you, something from that carpet. It reaches out to something miserable, something wretched in our souls, in all of our souls, as if a hungry child dying in a famine were stretching her hand to you but you have nothing that you can give her. Nothing to put in that outstretched, miserable, begging hand of hers. Nothing to make it better for her somehow. Such helplessness! Such hopelessness! It makes you want to beat your breast and tear apart your aching, bitter heart. Oh God! Oh God! One look and you want to weep for all the days that separate you from your grave. Mercy, my Lord! Mercy! I say, if the devil has such power to reach out to our souls, then there is no saving our souls at all. How could we? The soul isn't flesh, whose cravings, if left unchecked, can lead us straight to the devil's snares; it rather is the divine that has been breathed into each one of us, isn't it? It can only long for, it can only reach out to what is pure. And if the devil can concoct something that is so pure, then how are we to know the difference? How are we to save our souls? Besides, miracles, aren't they windows to God?

Windows to the everlasting and never born. Windows to the eternal and pure. Windows through which the soul longs to reach out to the Almighty and all-pure. That is why no devil can ever devise a miracle. That is why I say that carpet can never be wrought by the devil. Such work is beyond his damned reach. I say it must be the work of man. It has to be! Only a man is capable of a waylaid miracle, an inverted miracle. A man corrupted by grief. A man defiled by woe. A man lost in the dark depths of despair. Because it takes a man to blaspheme, not the devil. It is only a man who, when he is left with nothing else to blame for his misery, blames the divine order. The devil lost that consolation as soon as he refused to bow. A man it is. It must be. A man pitiable, no doubt, but he must yet be punished. Justice must be done. It has to be done before it is too late. The balance between heaven and hell has to be restored before it is too late. That is why the men are gathering. To punish ... But wait ... Now wait ... what is that? Wait! Wait! Do you hear that? That commotion? All those cries as if men are at war? ... Didn't I say there is anger in the air? Look! Look up there ... How many have gathered there! There, there ... Wait, wait, wait ... Let us stop here. As I said, those who cannot outrun the storm must keep their distance, at least. And that is precisely what we must do. I will, at least. There is no getting up there now. There is paying no obeisance at the shrine today. I am going back. You should too. Away from here. Away from them. To someplace safe. You must go to someplace safe till it gets better.'

31

The Pieces

This is it. This cave is all that the universe can afford as our refuge. This cave is what the world has shrunk to for us. Mine and Heemal's. There is no going outside. Everyone out there is after us. The fort is. The people must be. If not for the betrayal of Abli Bab, then for the sacrilege of the divine. And if for nothing else, they will hunt us down once they come to know that it is a defiled woman that I have brought to the threshold of the holy shrine. Everyone will want to hunt the runaway weaver and the missing whore. Everyone wants to punish the vain blasphemer and the fallen prostitute. Who did we offend more, I wonder? The fort, the people or the shrine?

'Let me out of here,' Heemal cries as she tries to get up and punch her way through the imperturbable wall of the cave. It isn't just fever that she is trying to escape from.

'Let me out. Let me out. There is not much time. I must hurry. Let me out. The cauldrons will not fill themselves. I need to get the water before it is too late. Why don't you understand? Let me out now.'

I rush to restrain her in my arms before she throws herself against the wall. 'Shush. Shush. It is all right. We will get out soon,' I try to calm her down. 'We will.'

'We will?'

'Yes. Yes. We will. We will. Soon, soon, my dear. Soon, we will.'

The consolation is too much for her. She collapses in my arms. She closes her eyes. Her breathing gets heavy and hard. She is panting for her life. The struggle continues for some time. She opens her eyes once again. But she isn't looking at me anymore. She stares across Time as the fever holds dozens of mirrors before her eyes.

'Father, Father, I did everything. I swear I did. Yet I failed. But I punished myself for the failure. Look, look, I sold myself. I did. But now I cannot take it anymore. Please forgive me. Please let me go now. I cannot bear it anymore. It is a boiling cauldron. There are worms crawling under my skin. And pus runs through my veins. I smell of rot and disgrace ...'

'Now, now, sweet little child. Shush ... shush ... go to sleep. Everything is fine. We are out of that blasted hell-hole.' I rock her in my arms. She closes her eyes once more. I run my fingers through the cascade of hair that tumbles down her head. Her breathing, still laboured, starts to ease. 'It wasn't your fault,' she murmurs softly, her eyes closed still. 'The bronze box was empty. It always has been. Empty. All empty. That is what the man from Samarqand had brought. An empty bronze box with a star. That is what he must have brought, after all. That is what he must have learnt, after all. An empty box to be filled with whatever you can. That is what he would have whispered to his worthy son. Fill the empty box, son. Fill it up with all that you are worth. And his worthy son. And his worthy son. Son after son. All of them sons. All of them worthy. They all filled it up. They filled the empty bronze box with all that they were worth. Every one of them did. Every one of them whispered this to his worthy son. And that is what you should have whispered to your worthy son. Fill it up with all that you are worth. Fill it up with colours that you are worthy of. Colours, father, that is what I was worthy of. Colours. That is what I filled the bronze box with. As best as I could, I filled that box with the bluest blue there is. Blue as the miracle of a summer sky. I filled the box with the bluest flowers of Niloufar. I whispered to myself, "I am worth all the colours. I am worthy." But it is you who should have whispered it to me. You should have told me to fill it up as best as I can. "Fill up this empty bronze box with whatever colour you can, my most worthy child." You should have whispered it in my ears. That is all that one can do. Fill up an empty box with as much as one can do. The Samarqand man did. My great-grandfather did. My grandfather did. I should have. We all should. The emptiness – it must be filled. It needs to be filled.'

'Yes, yes, we should. We all should. You already did. Of course you did. You filled it the best you could. You filled it with a colour true and bright.' Her face in my lap softens. I kiss her forehead. She winces a little. She opens her eyes. I try to smile.

'I did? I did?' she murmurs as she tries to smile back. 'I did. All those colours beautiful and bright. I loved them all. How many of them were on the wall! So many colours! So many colours! So many colours, but such little time. Such little time! Such little time!' the words are stuck on her tongue. She repeats them with increasing terror. 'Such little time! Such little time! Oh my God, we have such little time!'

'Now, now ... we will have enough time. Don't you worry about all that, my love.' I try to calm her down but she is no longer to be calmed. With a jerk, she frees herself from my arms.

'How am I to fill the emptiness in such little time?' she cries out aloud, 'How am I to fill all that emptiness in such little time?' she starts to shout, 'How will I? How will I?'

'Shush! Shush, my dear! We will find a way. We now have all the time.'

'You have. Yes, yes, you have and you will. You surely will. You surely must. I tried, but I couldn't. I was not a son. But you are. And you must. You have to fill up all the emptiness of the universe for both of us,' she says as she steps on the dismantled loom in her frenzy, its pieces held together by the white entangled threads of the warp. 'You have this to fill it all up. You have to. By God, you have to! You have this to weave to fill up all the emptiness,' she cries in excitement as she picks up a piece of the loom from the floor.

'Weave,' she cries as she collapses on the floor, 'Weave. Weave. Weave,' she commands me with her every breath. 'Weave. Weave. Weave.' Her wheezes fill up the cave.

'Weave. Weave. Weave.'

32

The Void

'Weave. Weave. Weave,' wheezes Heemal as she lies bundled on the ground, stiff and solemn. Or is it the blind old man wheezing in the dark? What difference does it make as long as it is the same whisper they wheeze out? *Weave. Weave. Weave.* The cave is full of these wheezes and I know it is futile to resist the call. The persistence of the wheezes knows no resistance. It never has. So I gather the pieces from the floor – the wooden beams and sideboards. I patch them up as best as I can. Though creaking and unsure, the loom is ready. It is sturdy enough to stretch and tighten the white threads of the untangled yarn across its frame.

'Weave. Weave. Weave,' the wheezes command as I stand before the loom like a prodigal son.

'I cannot,' I cry out loud. 'There is warp and there is weft but there is no thread left. There is nothing in here to tie the knots with.'

'Oh, but there is,' the wheezes whisper in my ear. 'Turn around and see.'

There is nothing but a pile of bones filling up a sack of skin behind me. That is what Heemal has been reduced to on the ground. Bones and skin with a mop of dishevelled hair on top of it. 'There, there ... There, you see,' the wheezes gloat. 'See, see ... There it is.'

'No, no. Not Heemal's hair!'

'But why not? She doesn't need it anymore. You do. Go on, take it.'

Those tresses, those bountiful tresses, a handful of them I gather in my palm. Tug and it comes off readily, as readily as leaves from a tree renouncing them in autumn.

'See, it doesn't even hurt. See, not even a pinch. It is all so easy. Take it. Take it all.'

I take it. I take it all. Handful after handful, I gather it. I gather what is left of Heemal. And I wind it all up into little balls.

'Now weave.'

Weave. Weave. Weave ... they all chant. I tie the first knot. A small knot. A tight knot. A black knot. It looks like a dot. It looks like a drop of black ink floating on the waves of a white sea. I tie one more knot. Again, a black knot. One more dot. The two coalesce into one. Black into black. It becomes impossible to tell the two apart.

I tie one more.

And another.

All of them black. All of them merge. I tie and tie. They keep on merging into one another. It is now a blotch of black on the loom. A blot of darkness that keeps growing. Growing and growing as it feeds on knot after knot. It outgrows the loom and creeps into the cave like a shadow stretching itself from all sides. It creeps all over me and spills into my eyes. It is all black. It is all encompassing. An eclipse that drowns everything into darkness except for a tiny blot of white. A dot of white small enough for just one more knot to be tied. One more knot and it will be an everlasting night.

I do it. I tie one more knot. As black a knot as the rest. But it is still there, this tiny drop of white. Maybe I was wrong. Maybe there is space for two. So, I tie one more knot.

Then I tie two more knots.

But it is still there, this stain of white. As big and as small as before. White and bright. A void of light. I tie and tie and tie and tie, but it remains there, this obstinate void of light. See how it mocks me – this insatiable void of light! It mocks every knot with which I try to fill it up. It mocks the last thread of Heemal's head with which I try to strangle it. It mocks every strand of hair that I pluck from my scalp to strangle it with. I tie and tie and it mocks and mocks.

Tie all the knots you can but you cannot fill up that void of light. That little void of white will remain unfulfilled, the wheezes whisper.

'But why? Why cannot I fill it up?'

Because there is always a knot left to be tied. There is always a knot after a knot after a knot. And as long as there is a knot to be tied, the void will remain.

'Why can't I tie a last knot and be done with it?'

Ha ha ha … if only it were so easy, my dear. If only it were up to you to decide which one would be your last knot.

'Then who is to decide? For God's sake, tell me who is to decide? If not me, then who will decide?'

'I think it is time for a story. A story to end it all.'

33

The Rope

It so happened that the mystic of mystics, that Sultan of Shaykhs, the exalted Junaid of Baghdad was walking with his disciples in the town bazaar. As they reached the market square, their eyes fell upon a man dragging a reluctant cow by a rope. 'Wait!' cried Junaid of Baghdad and the man with the cow brought his feet to a halt. 'Wait, my good man. Just a moment of yours. These disciples of mine, they need to learn something. And you and your cow, by the grace of God, they will find no better teachers than you two.'

The man was dumbfounded at the mystic's request. 'By all means,' he said with as much humility as he could muster while holding on tightly to the rope in his hands. Junaid thanked him and turned to his disciples. 'Now, my good fellows,' he said to them. 'Look at this man and look at his cow and look at that rope that joins the two of them. Look at them and answer me this: who is tied to whom? Is the cow tied to this man or is this man tied to the cow?'

And the disciples, trained as they were in the Way, had this to say in answer: 'What the eyes see, O wise Master, is that the cow is tied to the rope and the man holds the free end of the rope. What follows is but that the man tugs at the rope and the cow must follow. Thus, it so appears that it is the cow that is bound to the man.'

'Well then, let us see,' Junaid said with a smile. He asked for a pair of scissors and cut the rope with it at once. And no sooner did the rope snap than the cow made a dash for it. She ran as fast as she could and the man – angry and anxious – ran after her. 'My cow! My cow!' he cried as he ran after her.

'Now tell me,' said Junaid of Baghdad, 'who is tied to whom?'

34

The Last Knot

'Who is tied to whom? Now, that is a question that you must ask yourself. You ask it and you answer it and you will find your last knot.'

'Who is tied to whom?'

'Yes, yes. That is the question. What are you tied to?'

'Loom! Loom! Yes, yes I am bound to my loom.'

'Indeed, you are bound to your loom. But who is tied to whom?'

'Is the loom tied to me or am I tied to the loom?'

'Yes, yes, that is the question you need to answer.'

'Who is tied to whom?'

'Yes. Yes. Answer. Answer.'

'Answer. I need an answer. How do I find the answer?'

'How, indeed?'

'Rope! The rope! I must find the rope.'

'Yes. Yes. You must find the rope that binds you and your loom.'

'I must find the rope. I must find it and then cut it. Then we will know who is tied to whom.'

'Yes. Yes. Cut the rope. Cut the rope. We must cut the rope.'

'Yes. Yes, we must. But where is the rope?'

'Find it. Find it. Find that rope.'

'The rope binds us together – me and the loom.'

'Yes. Yes. It does.'

'What binds us together, me and the loom?'

'What does? What does?'

'Thumbs! My thumbs! By God, it is the thumbs. They bind us! My thumbs bind me and the loom!'

'Yes! Yes! They do. The thumbs. The thumbs.'

'My thumbs are the rope!'

'Yes. Yes. They are. They are.'

'I must cut them. I must cut the rope.'

'Yes. Yes. You must. No loose ends, remember?'

'Yes. Yes. I must cut my thumbs and I will have my answer in this darkness.'

'Yes, you must and you will. Just as it was foretold. You will cut your thumbs in darkness.'

'I must. I must. I will. I will.'

'Yes. Yes. Here, let me help you. Give me your hand. Stretch that thumb. Now, now, almost there.

Here, take this khour. Take it. Do it. Be done with it for once and for all. Yes, yes ... There ... There ... Done. Almost done ... There, it is done. Only one left now. This one here. Yes, yes, just like we did it already. Stretch this thumb. Here, here ... like this ... and yes, yes ... do it, do it ... yes, yes ... that is it. That is it. Now you are done.'

I am done. I am done, at last. Free! Free! Free, at last! I am free of the loom and the loom is free of me, at last. The carpet is free of us both.

But that abyss of white, that void of light; it is no void at all! I can see it now. It is a knot. A knot of light. It is my last knot. And yet the first as it weaves itself into one more knot. It spreads on the loom, the knot of light, it spreads like a spark of light at the end of a dark night. Knot after knot. Each one weaving another. Light spreading light. The light spreads itself across the loom into a bright carpet. A carpet glowing and throbbing on that loom. It shrugs itself free from the loom and lets itself glide into the dark cave. Uncertain but unafraid, the carpet hovers a little as if it were taking its first steps. Gradually, it steadies itself as it starts to float. It circles around me. Once, twice, before the crack in the rocks that forms the narrow mouth of the cave draws its attention and the gliding, floating carpet rushes there. It squeezes itself out and, for a brief moment, it is overwhelmed by the freedom that it floats into. It feels the wind flirting underneath it, the sweet pleasure of buoyancy coursing through its fibres. It doesn't resist the seduction of flight. It lets the waves of ecstasy carry it higher and higher. High up Haer Parbat. High up above the shrine. High, high, high up over the fort. It soars higher and higher. So high, it is beyond the reach of us all. Mine, the loom's, the cave's, the shrine's, the fort's, Haer Parbat's, the mountains'. It soars high up above and beyond us all. Through the clouds, it breaks into the vast emptiness of the cosmos. There it floats on the eternal waters of endless space and time – a boat of light ploughing its path through the great insouciant unknown ...

All that it leaves behind is its bright, blazing dream in the blind eyes of a thumbless weaver.